How to Win the MEXT Scholarship

Book 1 of the Mastering the MEXT Scholarship Guides

Travis Senzaki

For You,

You, with the big ideas and dreams; You, who will change the world; You, who just need a signpost to point you to the path to success.

Introduction to the Second Edition

Hello and congratulations on your decision to apply for the Japanese Government Monbukagakusho (MEXT) Scholarship for research students!

I have been working with MEXT Scholarship applicants for a decade, first as the primary point of contact for all MEXT scholarship applicants at a large, private university in Japan, where I handled over 500 applications-only about 10% were successful-and since then, I have helped thousands of MEXT scholarship applicants through my blogs, TranSenz and MyMEXTScholarship. I based this book on my experience and research into the behavior of successful applicants to help give your application the best possible chance of success.

I want to leverage that experience to help you, whether you just heard about the MEXT scholarship for the first time yesterday, or whether you're applying for the second or third time. No matter where you are in the application process, I am confident that I can offer experience and advice that will take your application to the next level and give you an advantage over other applicants. After all, as we'll cover more in the chapter on your application mindset, this application is competitive. It is a zero-sum game. There are only a certain number of slots to go around, and you need to be better than the competition to secure the scholarship you deserve.

I hope that does not frighten you. Instead, I hope it motivates you. As I said: **You deserve this scholarship**. And you can earn it, if you are prepared to put in the work.

Since I published the first edition of this book in 2018 (then titled *How to Apply for the MEXT Scholarship*), there have been a few changes to the application requirements and procedures. But the core of what you'll find in here-the application mindset and strategy-remains unchanged. If anything, a clear application strategy is *more* necessary, since the number of available slots has gone down and the competition is higher than ever. But, if you take the advice in the following pages to heart and put it into practice, I am confident that you can rise above the competition.

I'm excited to be with you here on your journey. Now, let's get started.

Travis Senzaki

https://mymextscholarship.com/

What This Book Will Do For You

This book explains the Japanese government Monbuka-gakusho (MEXT) scholarship, outlines the application procedure, and helps you develop the mindset and specific application strategy to succeed. It is based on over a decade of experience working with thousands of applicants to bring you the most comprehensive information possible.

This is the first book in my series of guides on the MEXT scholarship for research students (that means "graduate students" and is one of many frustratingly confusing terms). It's also the most important one, regardless of where you are in your application journey.

Over the last 13 years (and counting), I have helped thousands of applicants apply for the scholarship through my blog, but until the first edition of *How to Apply for the MEXT Scholarship,* I had not written a guide that will take you start-to-finish through the application process. This book and series takes the best of my articles, plus additional research and exercises, to walk you through the process step-by-step.

With this series of guides, you can pick up wherever you are in the application process, find tips and experience from past applicants, as well as my research, and follow through to the end. But, regardless of where you are, I encourage you not to skip the chapters on the Successful Applicant Mindset and Application Strategy later in this book.If you get the mindset and strategy down, then even if you don't read the rest of the books in the series, you will have the most important tools you need to find the necessary information through other sources. (The other books will be a shortcut for you, though!)

In this first book, I will introduce the scholarship, explain the mindset you need to succeed, help you figure out if you are eligible to apply, and help you create your application strategy that will distinguish you from other applicants and maximize your chances to earn the scholarship.

The first chapter covers the basics: the scholarship categories, the different ways to apply, and the scholarship benefits. I'll explain how to get started with each kind of application process, and the pros and cons of applying for the embassy-recommended scholarship and the university-recommended scholarship.

In the second chapter, I will describe one of the most important, fundamental subjects in this entire series: Your application mindset. I will help you understand how you need to approach the scholarship, including the mistakes many applicants make that eliminate them from contention, and the habits you can adopt to stand out as a professional, desirable applicant.

Next, chapter three explains eligibility requirements for the scholarship. I will explain the eligibility criteria in detail, including the eligibility criteria that are not released or explained in English and the ones that cause confusion each year. The most challenging eligibility criteria to understand is the GPA requirement, since MEXT uses a 3-point scale that is not used anywhere else in the world (including by Japanese universities). I will help you convert your grades to that scale.

Once we have covered the basics of applying and determined that you are eligible, in the fourth and final chapter, I will explain how to create your application strategy. Even if you get nothing else out of this book, that chapter will set you on your path to success.

The other books in this series cover:

2. How to Write a Scholarship-Winning Field of Study and Research Program Plan

The Field of Study and Research Program Plan is the most important document in your application package. In book 2,

I explain how to develop a research proposal based on your interest, experience, and the application strategy that you will create in this book, and how to write it up in a way that will appeal to MEXT Scholarship reviewers.

https://mymext.com/getmms2

3. How to Find your best Degree Program and Advisor for the MEXT Scholarship

How to find out which Japanese universities offer degree programs and have professors specialized in your research field, plus when and how to contact them.

https://mymext.com/getmms3

These three books should set you up with everything you need for success in your scholarship application! Read on to the end of this book for information on how you can get books 2 and 3 at a discount.

What You Need to Do

I will share everything I know about the MEXT scholarship process and best practices for the application, but let's get this out of the way first:

You are going to have to do the work.

There is no substitute for hard work and research in this application process. I don't teach cheap gimmicks or ways to cheat the system (I'm not aware of any). I teach a systematic way to strengthen your application and increase your appeal to the professors and government staff who will review your application. But it is up to you to put those steps into practice.

This book, and the rest of the series, are packed with tips and steps to make your application stronger. It may seem overwhelming if you look at them all at once, but approach each tip one at a time and it should be more manageable. Each step you choose to implement improves your chances and each step you ignore gives your competition the chance to pass you by. It is up to you to decide how much you really want this scholarship and how hard you are going to work.

Still with me? Good!

Academic Support

There are a few other assets you need to bring, starting with your academic background. There is nothing I (or even you, most likely) can do about your grades in your last degree. The higher they are, the better your chances will be. If they're below the mark that we discuss in the chapter on eligibility, then you can't even apply. So, grades are on you.

If you're the kind of person who is willing to invest in yourself by buying a scholarship application guidebook, I assume you're also the kind of person who invested in yourself by earning excellent grades.

You will also want to have access to an expert in your academic field, such as your advisor from your last degree. I am an expert in the application process, but chances are good that I do not have any expertise in your academic field. While I will guide you through the process of crafting a Field of Study and Research Program Plan in Book 2 of this series, I cannot help you evaluate your particular research topic or give advice specific to your field from and academic perspective.

Finally, if you are not a native English speaker, you will want to find one among your friends who can help review your application and Field of Study and Research Program Plan later on. I offer application reviews for a fee, including content and language advice, but during the application season, I cannot always keep up with the number of requests, especially around the application deadline.

Aside from the grades and willingness to put in hard work, you won't need any of the things above to make it through this first book, so while you're assembling your team of experts, let's get started!

Downloadable Exercise Worksheets and Resources

Each chapter has an accompanying series of exercises that will help you work through the contents as you go along. I highly recommend that you complete them as you go. I have compiled the exercise questions at the end of the chapter, but you can also download them in advance from the link below in worksheet format. I highly recommend that you download them, print them, and fill them out as you go along.

https://mymext.com/bonusmms1

Along with those worksheets, you will also find the TranSenz GPA Spreadsheet and conversion charts that we'll refer to in Chapter 3, plus links to all of the resources that I refer to throughout the book, so that you don't have to type out the URLs one by one. You will also be signed up for the companion email course, where I will send you a series of emails that go along with the book to help keep you on pace and any future updates to the contents of this book or the bonus materials as the scholarship process changes or I learn more from other applicants' experiences.

Please go download those worksheets now and complete them as you read along for the most benefit. I will also include a link to the worksheets after each chapter and all of the exercises at the back of the book, but the companion email course works best if you start it from the beginning.

Contents

Understanding the MEXT Scholarship

The MEXT Scholarship is a scholarship program for international students offered by the Japanese Ministry of Education, Culture, Sports, Science and Technology (MEXT). It is available at various levels, from a one-year undergraduate study abroad program all the way up through graduate degrees.

This book and series are for applicants for the graduate-level scholarship.

Benefits of the Scholarship

As of the time of publication, the MEXT Scholarship offers:

- Complete tuition exemption for the duration of your studies,

- A stipend of 143,000 - 145,000 yen/month, depending on your degree level, plus a cost-of-living adjustment of 2,000 - 3,000 yen/month depending on where you live in Japan,

- One free round-trip international flight ticket between your home country and Japan, to bring you here for the start of your studies and get you home after you finish, and

- Payment of entrance exam and matriculation fees.

You can even extend your scholarship award period. You can start as a master's level research student, then go on to a master's degree, followed by a PhD. It is possible to extend the scholarship each time you move up to the next level to cover your entire duration of study. That could be over 10 million yen in scholarship stipend payments, and that's not even counting the value of the tuition and flight tickets.

That's a pretty generous offer by any standard. The stipend is enough to live on, even in Tokyo. In rural areas, I have even seen students with families cover the cost of living for their spouse and child with their stipend.

Purpose of the Scholarship

Of course, the Japanese government is not just being generous. This is not a handout or even a need-based scholarship. Your financial situation and need are not factors in the scholarship selection process.

The scholarship is an investment by the Japanese government and has specific goals for graduates of the program.

Specifically, the program intends to:

- Educate future leaders in politics and education who will understand and be sympathetic toward Japan as they advance through their careers;

- Educate students who will return home and become ambassadors for their Japanese universities, contributing to recruiting more students, including self-financed students, to study in Japan in the future;

- Benefit Japan's economy, both directly by having international students in the country and indirectly by educating future business leaders who will keep connections with Japan throughout their career;

- Develop ambassadors for Japanese culture who will spread interest in the country once they return home; and others.

The "leaders in politics and education" goal has had the strongest results in Asia, especially ASEAN, where a Japanese education offers an advantage over many domestic programs. In these countries, past graduates from Japanese universities, especially MEXT scholars, have risen to senior government posts and leadership within local universities.

In developed countries in North America, Western Europe, and Oceania, the "developing Japanese cultural ambassadors" goal has a higher impact. These countries' higher education systems are often stronger than Japan's, so a degree from a Japanese university does not offer the same career advantages.

Keep these outcomes in mind as you go through your scholarship application. You will want to take every opportunity to show the scholarship reviewers that you have the clear potential to deliver the value they seek on their investment.

Scholarship Availability

The MEXT Scholarship for Research Students is the largest category of scholarships offered by MEXT, but that doesn't mean that the opportunities are plentiful. MEXT does not publish the total number of scholarship slots available in each country each year, but we can estimate the number based on official government statistics.

Total MEXT Scholarship Slots and Estimated New Slots

Each year, MEXT requires universities to report the total number of international students enrolled and compiles annual statistics on the state of education. The data does not show the number of new MEXT scholars, but it gives us enough information to make an educated guess. For this calculation, I am going to use the data collected in May 2019 (e-Stat, "Number of International Students by Major (Graduate School)"), before the COVID-19 Pandemic and lengthy border closures.

I'll explain my math below, but my estimate for new graduate scholarship slots from 2019 is:

- Non-degree students: 773

- Master's degree/ Professional degree: 2,370

- Doctoral degree: 763

- Total: 3,906

Here's the explanation:

In 2019, there were 773 non-degree MEXT scholars and 7,009 degree-seeking MEXT scholars at the graduate level.

The data does not differentiate between master's- and doctoral-level MEXT scholars. However, there is data available for the total numbers of master's, doctoral, and professional degree students for that year. To estimate, I will use the same ratio: 67.6% master's and professional, 32.4% doctoral. That gives us 4,739 master's scholars and 2,270 doctoral scholars.

If we assume an even distribution in each year, we can then assume that 2,370 new master's MEXT scholars and 763 new doctoral MEXT scholars enrolled that year.

This number is also consistent with a report from May 2015 that showed 4,042 new graduate-level MEXT scholars that year.

Slot Distribution

Although there are around 4,000 slots available, you are competing for one of a much smaller number.

There are two scholarship application processes: the Embassy-Recommended MEXT Scholarship and University-Recommended MEXT Scholarship, which we'll cover in more detail later on. Slots are further divided among individual countries or embassies for the Embassy-Recommended MEXT Scholarship application and among universities in Japan for the University-Recommended MEXT Scholarship. There might be only 2 slots available to your local consulate (Embassy-Recommended MEXT Scholarship) or 3 slots available to the university where you want to study (University-Recommended MEXT Scholarship).

In other words, expect intense competition and be prepared to take every step in your power to give yourself an advantage over other applicants. That is what we will do for the rest of this book and series.

Other Types of MEXT Scholarships

I mentioned earlier that there are other types of MEXT scholarships that are not covered by this book. While these scholarships are not relevant to you, I will list them here in case you come across the terms later and want to know if they are relevant.

- **Undergraduate Students:** For current high school students between 17-22 years of age when they start their degrees who want to complete their bachelor's degree in Japan. This scholarship also includes a year of Japanese language studies before the degree starts, then MEXT will assign students to a Japanese-taught degree program at its discretion. Based on data from 2023, there are approximately 310 slots open to applicants from 200 countries. The only application method is Embassy-Recommended MEXT Scholarship or through PGP programs offered by universities.

- **Colleges of Technology:** In Japan, Colleges of Technology are a separate category of higher education institution from universities. They award a three-year technical degree that is equivalent to an associate's degree. As of 2023, there were approximately 72 slots available per year. While 40 countries are eligible, the 2023 data shows that only 26 countries were represented and about 85% of scholarship recipients were from East or Southeast Asia (e-Stat, "International students by nationality and associated department"). Like the undergraduate program, this scholarship includes a year of Japanese language preparation before students take their programs entirely in Japanese. The only application method is via the Japanese embassy.

- **Specialized Training Colleges:** Similar to Colleges of Technology, this program is for high school graduates, but the education level is lower (it awards a diploma, not an associate's degree) and the fields of study differ. While Colleges of Technology focus on engineering-type programs, Specialized Training Colleges include fields like nutrition, education, business, fashion, and culture. Since Specialized Training Colleges are not part of higher education (they are secondary education), I could not find statistics for the number of students. You can safely assume it is less than Colleges of Technology and similarly limited in terms of countries. The only application method is via the Japanese embassy.

- **Japanese Studies Scholarship:** This is a one-year scholarship program for undergraduate exchange students who will spend one year of their degree in Japan. As the name suggests, it only applies to students majoring in Japanese studies (Japanese language and culture). Students from 74 countries were eligible for 190 total slots, as of 2015. It is only available at a predetermined list of universities in Japan. It is possible to apply via the Japanese embassy or via one of the designated universities in Japan.

- **Teacher's Training:** This is the only other graduate-level MEXT Scholarship program. The scholarship duration is for up to one-and-a-half years of special training in a teacher's training program and may include six months of Japanese language training if necessary. There were only 89 slots available to applicants from 64 countries, as of 2015.

- **Young Leaders' Program:** The Young Leaders' Program is the most restricted category and you cannot choose to apply to it. It is only available in 27 developing countries in Asia and it requires formal nomination from an official organization in your country.

The MEXT Scholarship for Research Students has more slots available, is open to applicants from more countries, and is much more valuable. Graduate education, when you are most specialized in your discipline, gives you the best opportunity to make the most of the resources available to you in Japan.

Categories of the MEXT Scholarship for Research Students

Although this is called the MEXT Scholarship for "Research Students", *you can apply for a degree program through this scholarship*. For more about definitions of terms, including the two different meanings of "Research Students" please see Appendix B.

Now, let's break down what it means to be a research student, a master's degree student, or a PhD student under the MEXT scholarship.

Research Student

Everyone who earns the scholarship is a *"kenkyūsei"* research student in the sense that they are a graduate-level student. However, you can also be a *"hiseikisei"* research student (or non-degree student) at a university.

For university enrollment status, research student (*hiseikisei*) means "non-degree" student. Most times, this is a student who is affiliated with a particular master's or PhD program, but has not yet passed the entrance exam to start their degree. Many MEXT scholars start as research students for a semester, or up to two full years, depending on their academic ability or on the policy of the university.

Applicants for the Embassy-Recommended MEXT Scholarship often spend their first semester in Japan in an intensive Japanese language program to help teach some basics for everyday life. Students in this program are research students.

You may also start as a research student if your university requires you to take an in-person entrance exam in Japan before enrolling in the degree program. You might also be a research student if you arrive in the wrong semester to start the degree. (Some degree programs will only matriculate new students in either the spring or the fall.)

The second type of research student, a "pure" research student, is enrolled in a graduate degree program overseas and only plans to come to Japan to conduct their field research. They have no intention of matriculating to a degree program at a Japanese university. This type of student is almost unheard-of in the MEXT scholarship program and is not allowed in the University-Recommended MEXT Scholarship.

You can be a research student at either the master's degree level or PhD level, depending on the degree program that you plan to enter.

There is nothing negative about being a research student. Unless you have a time limit to finish your degree and return to your home country, I recommend spending a semester as a research student. This allows you to get used to the Japanese university system and living in a new country before you go "on the clock" for your degree program.

Roles of a Research Student

As a research student, your activities are up to your academic advisor's discretion. However, you will probably attend classes and conducting research, just like a degree-seeking student. You will need to spend a minimum of 10 hours per week in class or active research, as that is the minimum requirement to maintain your student visa. You will have all the rights and privileges of an enrolled student during this time, too.

While you will not be enrolled in the degree program yet, you should be able to earn credits and "transfer" them later to count toward your degree after you matriculate.

If you enroll in the intensive Japanese language program under research student status, you will not take content courses, but you may meet with your advisor to plan and start work on your research.

Benefits and Duration as a Research Student

As a research student, your tuition is waived (for national universities) or covered by MEXT (for public or private universities), as with degree-seeking students. Your stipend is 143,000 yen per month, as of 2023, plus a possible

2,000-3,000 yen per month cost-of-living adjustment, in some areas.

You can remain a research student for a maximum of two years, if you start your studies in Japan in April, or one-and-a-half years if you start in September/October. That time limit includes the time spent in Japanese language studies, if applicable.

By the end of your time limit as a research student, you must pass the degree program entrance exam and simultaneously apply to extend your MEXT scholarship. Otherwise, you would have to return home at the end of your research student period. It is possible to attempt the entrance exam to your degree program multiple times during this period, but you must also apply to extend your scholarship at the same time.

Degree-Seeking Student

Master's, PhD, and Professional Degree Programs

You can enroll in a degree program or start as a research student and extend your studies to a degree program. Starting as a research student and extending is the common approach, especially under the Embassy-Recommended MEXT Scholarship.

There are two degree levels and two special categories of degrees. The levels are, of course, master's and doctoral, as explained in the definitions in the Preface.

The first special category is professional degrees, which include MBAs (Master of Business Administration), LLM (Master of Laws), JD (Juris Doctorate - law degree), MD (Medical Doctor), etc, These are not academic degrees, but are career-focused graduate programs. They can be at the master's or doctoral level, as specified in the degree title.

The other is a five-year integrated doctorate, which is a master's and doctoral program combined, but does not award an interim master's degree after the first two years. For scholarship purposes, you would be a master's degree student for the first two years of the five-year program and a PhD student for the final three years. Just like any other student extending from a master's to a doctorate, you would need to apply for a scholarship extension in the middle. You would not be granted a five-year scholarship from the start.

At both the master's and doctoral level in Japan, you must conduct original research. There is no such thing as a "taught master's", where you would just attend classes to earn your degree. At the PhD level, however, there are programs that are purely research PhDs and others that will require some classes. You will need to research your specific program for more details.

Degree Program Duration

In Japan, you have two years to complete a master's and three years to complete a doctoral program. If you do not complete the degree within that time, you would not be able to extend your scholarship. (In fact, as we'll cover later on, as soon as it becomes apparent that you cannot complete your degree in that amount of time, you would lose your scholarship immediately.) If you are unsure whether you can complete your degree in that amount of time, start as a research student to give yourself a head start on your requirements.

Some doctoral degrees in the fields of medicine, dentistry, veterinary science, and pharmacy are 4-year programs. In the Japanese system, these programs follow after a six-year undergraduate degree. If you earn the MEXT Scholarship for one of those programs, you would have the necessary four years to complete your degree. You would also need special additional certification to participate in any clinical sessions. MD programs would also require you to be fluent in Japanese, since the national certification exam is in Japanese and is hard to pass, even for native speakers.

Benefits as a Master's- or Doctoral-level Student

Your tuition is waived or paid for by MEXT. The stipend amount is 144,000 yen per month for master's-level students and 145,000 yen per month for doctoral-level students, as of 2023, though it is subject to change. Students at both levels may receive the 2,000-3,000 yen per month cost-of-living adjustment, depending on the university's location.

Which Should You Apply For?

Applicants often ask me whether they have a better chance of success if they apply as a research student or as a degree-seeking student right off the bat. As long as both options are available to you, the answer is that it doesn't affect your chances.

If you have a choice, I recommend you to start as a research student. This is more to increase your chances of success *after* you start your studies.

As mentioned above, once you start your degree program, you have a limited amount of time to complete it. Your first semester in Japan is going to be difficult. You will need to adjust to a new culture and a new education system, set up your housing, and get used to daily life. If you will invite your family to move to Japan to join you during that semester, that would take even more time and energy as you get them settled.

It's better to give yourself flexibility to do that while you are not "on the clock" for your degree. You lose nothing by being a research student first.

Sometimes, though, you won't have a choice. If you're applying through the University-Recommended MEXT Scholarship, some programs *only* accept research students and some only accept degree-seeking students. If you make the wrong selection in those cases, you'll show the university that you didn't care enough to read the applications guidelines, and that will hurt your chances.

For the University-Recommended MEXT Scholarship, except for some PGP Programs, you can only arrive in Japan starting in the fall semester (September or October). Since some degree programs only accept new students matriculating in the spring, you would have to start as a research student for those programs. University-Recommended MEXT Scholarship programs that accept new matriculating students in the fall are unlikely to offer research student status.

If you are applying for the Embassy-Recommended MEXT Scholarship, then you will almost certainly spend your first semester in an intensive Japanese language program, which is considered research student status. The university decides whether to place you in this program. If your Japanese ability is below N2 level, then it's safe to assume they will want you to take that program. The Japanese language program intends to get you up to speed for day-to-day Japanese so that you can take care of yourself, your shopping, your banking, your rent, etc. It will not teach you academic Japanese for studying.

Consider that language program semester when you decide when you would like to arrive in Japan and when you would start studies in your actual program. If you want to start your degree program in the fall, then you could arrive in the spring to take the Japanese language program and then matriculate directly to the degree in the fall. Alternatively, you could arrive in the fall, spend one semester in the Japanese language program and one as a research student, then start your degree a full year after you arrive in Japan. That's the course of action that I recommend.

The last thing to consider in your decision is your prospective advisor's opinion. If your advisor wants you to start in a particular semester, their input will override your preference.

Ultimately, remember that your arrival semester has more to do with your success after arrival than it does with your success in the application process.

Application Process Overview

Now that we've discussed the different levels of degree that you can apply for, let's go into a little more depth about the two application processes and their differences.

The two application processes are the Embassy-Recommended MEXT Scholarship and University-Recommended MEXT Scholarship. The process you choose will affect your application process, from the timing, to the paperwork, to how many universities you'll need to contact.

Perhaps most significantly, it will impact your odds of success.

I describe each process in detail, including instructions for each form and document, application steps, and specific advice to increase your chances of success in articles on my website (**https://mymextscholarship.com**). I update those articles each year, so please read those for the most recent information. For now, I will explain the basics of both processes to help you choose which one is best for you.

(Hint: I recommend starting with whichever comes first, depending on when you read this. So pay particular attention to the timeline for each.)

Embassy-Recommended MEXT Scholarship

Most MEXT Scholarship winners earn their scholarships by applying through the Japanese embassy or consulate in their home countries. While the process is longer and more complex than the University-Recommended MEXT Scholarship, it offers the greatest chance of success for most prepared applicants.

In almost all cases, I recommend applying for the Embassy-Recommended MEXT Scholarship first, unless it is too late for you to apply as you are reading this. (See the timeline below.)

Let's start by looking at some advantages and disadvantages.

Advantages and Disadvantages

For most applicants, the Embassy-Recommended MEXT Scholarship offers more advantages than disadvantages. Including:

- **Save on test fees:** You do not need to submit TOEFL or JLPT test scores to apply for the Embassy-Recommended MEXT Scholarship. Instead, you will take language proficiency tests at the embassy after you pass the document screening. However, you may need to submit language proficiency test scores later when you apply to universities for a Letter of Acceptance after the Primary Screening.

- **Save on postage fees:** No need to pay for expensive international mail services.

- **More slots available:** In almost all cases, you will compete for a larger number of slots than you would if you applied for the University-Recommended MEXT Scholarship.

- **Compete with your country:** You do not need to worry about differences in the grading system between countries giving particular applicants an advantage. Depending on how well-known the MEXT Scholarship is in your country, there might be a smaller competition pool, too.

There are two primary disadvantages to the Embassy-Recommended MEXT Scholarship: Time and interference.

- **Time:** The Embassy-Recommended MEXT Scholarship application process starts between April to June of the year *before* you plan to start your studies, so you need to start well in advance. In some cases, you'll start your application more than a year before you graduate. For example, if you want to start your studies in October 2025, you would start your application no later than April 2024. And you should prepare even earlier.

- **Local government interference:** Your home country government can impose additional screenings and conditions. For example, it might limit the fields of study available (India, Philippines), impose a pre-screening and compel you to return home immediately after graduation (Mexico), or have local government officials sit in on your interview (Malaysia). This can add complexity to your application process. But if you are prepared for this challenge, you may have an advantage over the applicants who are not.

That last comment is something important to keep in mind, especially as we turn to your mindset in a future chapter. Whenever you feel tempted to see something as a disadvantage or challenge, realize that the same challenge applies to all applicants. If you know about it and prepare for it in advance, then it becomes an advantage for you.

Unless, of course, you are competing against the Prime Minister's daughter, or something like that. In that case, there's nothing you can do. But I hope that is not the case for you.

Application Timeline

So, when do you need to start your application? At least a year before you plan to start your degree in Japan.

Specific dates will vary by country, so be sure to check with the Japanese embassy or consulate where you plan to apply. What follows is a general overview of the application timeline. The same timeline holds true whether you plan to arrive for the spring (April) or fall (September/October) semester.

1. Determine your field of study and research question. Start researching and drafting your Field of Study and Research Program Plan.
   When: October-December, 2 years before arrival in Japan
   See book 2 of this series: How to Write a Scholarship-Winning Field of Study and Research Program Plan (**https://mymext.com/getmms2**)
   *This is not a strict deadline, just a recommendation.

2. Identify your target universities and prospective advisors in Japan. Finish the first draft of your Field of Study and Research Program Plan and start reaching out to professors to establish relationships.
   When: January-March, 1 year before arrival in Japan
   See book 3 of this series: How to Find your best Degree Program and Advisor for the MEXT Scholarship (**https://mymext.com/getmms3**) for more details.
   *This is not a strict deadline, just a recommendation.

3. Application guidelines and forms released on MEXT and embassy websites. Start your application!
   When: April-May, 1 year before arrival in Japan

4. Application submission deadline.
   When: May-June, 1 year before arrival in Japan
   *This is the first real deadline

5. Document screening, language proficiency tests, embassy interview.
   When: May-July, 1 year before arrival in Japan

6. Results of Primary Screening Released: Congratulations! You have passed the biggest hurdle. Almost all applicants who pass the primary screening earn the scholarship. Start contacting universities for Letters of Provisional Acceptance (LoPA).
   When: July-early August, 1 year before arrival in Japan

7. Deadline to contact universities to ask for an LoPA.
   When: Early August, 1 year before arrival in Japan
   Specific deadline varies each year. See the application guidelines for details.

8. Deadline to submit LoPAs to the Japanese embassy or consulate.
   When: September-October, 1 year before arrival in Japan
   This is the typical range, but your embassy or consulate will set their own deadline, so please consult with them for details.

9. Secondary Screening (a.k.a. The Long Wait, Part I).
When: September-October, 1 year before arrival in Japan
Most applicants will not receive confirmation of passing the Secondary Screening from your embassy. They will proceed to the next step.

10. University Placement Process (a.k.a. The Long Wait, Part II).
When: November-December, 1 year before arrival in Japan
During this time, you might receive unofficial notification of your successful secondary screening and placement from the university. They are not supposed to tell you anything, but sometimes they need to contact you for additional details.

11. Final Results and University Placement released!
When: January-February, year of arrival

12. Visa, travel arrangements, and packing for your trip to Japan!
When (Spring Semester Arrivals): January-March, year of arrival
When (Fall Semester Arrivals): July-September, year of arrival

13. Settle in to life in Japan in your degree program or language studies. Establish your day-to-day life and

routines. Start thinking about inviting your family to join you, if applicable.

When (Spring Semester Arrivals): April, year of arrival

When (Fall Semester Arrivals): September-October, year of arrival

If you start your scholarship as a non-degree student (either in the Japanese language program or at your university), then you will need to apply to extend your scholarship to cover the degree program.

Don't panic! There's a lot of work ahead of you, but you don't need to tackle everything at once. The entire purpose of this guide series is to break the process down into small, straightforward steps, to help ease you through applying with minimal stress and confusion!

Document Submission and Screening

The Call for Applications should come from the Japanese embassy or consulate in your home country around April. Remember that this is the call for applications for the scholarship starting a full year or more later!

That announcement should include the specific applications procedures for your country, including the application deadlines, as well as all the forms you need. I have articles on my website that I update each year covering the forms and procedures, so please refer to those for the most recent information:

https://mymext.com/erms

To find the website for the nearest Japanese embassy or consulate, refer to the Japanese Ministry of Foreign Affairs web page below:[1]

https://mymext.com/embassies

(I will also list all the websites and other resources again in the back of this book.)

Depending on your country, you may have a single embassy, multiple consulates, or no physical Japanese embassy at all. If you have a single embassy, then your process is straightforward, but in the other cases, you're going to need to do a little more work.

If there are multiple Japanese consulates, then it is likely that each one serves only a specific area. You do not get to choose which consulate to apply to. Apply to the one that is responsible for the area you live in. Check their websites for further details.

---

1. Note: All links in this book go through my website and redirect to the appropriate page. This is to make it easier to type, if necessary, and to allow me to update the redirects if the destination URLs change in the future. If you find a broken link, please let me know by adding a comment at https://mymext.com/mms1

There may be no Japanese embassy in your country. This is most often the case in areas that have been hit by war, or countries where there are minimal relations with the local government. In that case, you will still find a link to your country's embassy on the page above, but that embassy may be in a different country. For example, the Japanese embassy in Yemen is located in Riyadh, Saudi Arabia. Yemeni applicants would have to apply through that embassy.

As long as the Japanese government recognizes your country, there will be an embassy to serve you.

Another important resource is MEXT's own web page for the scholarship:

https://mymext.com/mextofficial

In the past, MEXT only posted information about the Embassy-Recommended MEXT Scholarship on its own website, linked above, which is only in Japanese. Since 2020, though, the guidelines have also been available each year on JASSO's official "Study in Japan" website in English. In most years, JASSO updates the guidelines before MEXT or the individual embassies do, so it's a great resource to check often. You can also find all the required forms there.

https://mymext.com/sijg

Check the embassy's website, JASSO's Study in Japan site, and MEXT's page at least once per day from April 1 until the MEXT scholarship application information becomes available. You can add those pages to the start-up tabs in your internet browser, or use a service that checks websites for changes and notifies you. I use visualping.io, as mentioned in Appendix D.

Language Proficiency Tests

If you pass the document screening, the embassy or consulate will contact you to participate in the Japanese and English language proficiency tests. Sometimes, you may have the interview (see the next section) scheduled on the same day.

You are required to submit the Japanese test, even if you are applying for a program taught in English. Even if have no Japanese ability, do not turn in the test blank. Take a guess at the questions. I have heard of applicants who were rejected during the Secondary Screening because their Japanese language tests were blank! If you do have some ability, do your best on this test. It may be a factor in determining whether you spend your first semester in Japan in the intensive Japanese language program. Some embassies also prioritize applicants with Japanese language ability, since it shows a higher level of interest in Japan and preparedness to live there.

Of course, the Japanese test is essential if you are planning to apply to a program taught in Japanese!

For most people reading this book, the English language proficiency test is more important, even though it is technically optional. It is *not* optional if you are applying to a degree program taught in English. Because of bureaucratic rigidity, you may even be required to take this test if English is your native (and only) language. The test can be deceptively difficult for native speakers, since it is for second-language speakers who study English from a different, more technical approach. So, do not skimp on your preparation! At least read through the sample tests I have collected from past years at the link below.

In countries where English is not the primary language, these tests can cull a significant portion of the applicants. In Thailand in 2017, for example, there were separate written and oral tests and only 34% of applicants passed the written test and moved on to the oral.

MEXT has made past tests available so that you can practice in advance. Whether you are a native or second-language speaker, you should take advantage of them. The tests are the embassy's last chance to reduce the number of applicants before the interviews. Since interviews are time intensive, the embassy will be motivated to reduce the number of applicants beforehand.

You can find old tests at the following link:

https://mymext.com/exams

Interview

Once you complete the language tests, the final stage of the embassy's Primary Screening process is the interview. Depending on your country, this may be on the same day as the language proficiency tests.

Most times, the interview is 20 minutes long, and you will face anywhere from 2 to 5 interviewers in a panel. Interviewers may include embassy staff (bureaucrats interested in building relationships between Japan and your home country), officials from your government (interested in how your studies will benefit your country) and/or professors in your field from a local university (interested in the academic merit of your proposal). You need to be prepared to answer questions about your Field of Study and Research Program Plan, your plans for after graduation, and your knowledge of Japan—from your interests to how you will adapt to life there—keeping the interests of each of the interviewer types in mind.

The majority of the interview should be in English. If you have stated in your application documents that you have some Japanese ability, the interviewers may ask you a few questions in Japanese to test your ability. On some rare occasions, I have also heard or part of the interview being conducted in the local language of your country.

You may face a challenging interviewer, one who seems out to get you or seems to be out to get you. Keep in mind that the interviewer is probably behaving the same way toward all applicants. They may think it's their job to see how you react to stress and be deliberately antagonistic. Don't let that get you down!

I have an article about how to prepare for the interview that I update with questions that applicants share on my website at the link below:

https://mymext.com/embint

The interview is your "Final Exam" at the embassy. Passing the interview stage means passing the Primary Screening, which all but guarantees you will receive the scholarship.

Requesting Letters of Provisional Acceptance

Once you have passed the Primary Screening at the embassy or consulate, you are almost certain to be selected as a scholarship winner, but there is one key step remaining. You must contact up to two universities and professors from your Placement Preference Form to apply for a Letter of Provisional Acceptance. Once you have secured at least one Letter of Provisional Acceptance and submitted it to your embassy or consulate, then your active part of the application process is complete.

You are not required to apply only to the universities in your Placement Preference Form. If you have determined that another university and professor is better suited to your research since you submitted the form, then you can apply there instead. You can change the Placement Preference Form when you resubmit it with your Letters of Provisional Acceptance. For more information about applying for Letters of Provisional Acceptance, please see the most up-to-date articles on my website:

https://mymext.com/lopa

You should request Letters of Provisional Acceptance immediately after you learn you have passed the Primary Screening. Ideally, you would have already been in contact with your prospective advisor, but this will be your first opportunity to officially request a Letter of Provisional Acceptance.

You can find more information about how to find the best university and advisor for your research and how to contact them in the third book in this series.

Depending on your country, it could be anywhere from early July to mid-August when you receive your notification of passing the Primary Screening. Regardless of the timing, do not delay in contacting universities. Each year, there is a strict deadline in August for you to contact universities to request your Letter of Provisional Acceptance. If you contact them after the deadline, they are not allowed to accept your application. You should also consider that August is summer vacation in Japan and it may be harder to get a quick response from universities. Universities are supposed to return the results of their screening to you in approximately one month, but if you send your request when the university is closed, the clock starts when they receive the application after reopening.

Your embassy or consulate will tell you the deadline to submit your Letters of Placement Acceptance to them. Once you have turned them in, that is the last part of the process for you. The only thing remaining is a maddening wait for 4-5 months for the final results and your placement.

Secondary Screening

Once you submit your Letters of Provisional Acceptance to the embassy or consulate, they will forward all of your application materials to MEXT for the Secondary Screening.

The Secondary Screening is essentially MEXT double-checking the embassy's work. They will make sure the embassy did not make any mistakes and that you are not researching something like weapons technology, etc. They will also check if you have a criminal history in Japan or a history of being deported. It is not a competitive screening. The only time I have heard of applicants being rejected during the Secondary Screening was in 2019, when MEXT reduced the number of scholarship slots *after* the Primary Screening was over in some countries. This is unlikely to happen again.

MEXT and the embassy will say that your scholarship is not yet guaranteed at this point and that there is a chance of being eliminated, but that is just bureaucratic nonsense. They can't say anything else until the final approval is complete. In almost all cases, you do not need to worry about it.

The embassy may contact you to let you know you have passed the secondary screening (rare), or they may wait and not contact you at all until after the final university placement is complete.

University Placement

Once MEXT determines that your application meets its standards, they will contact universities from your Placement Preference Form to ask them to accept you.

Typically, MEXT will contact the universities in the priority order that you listed them. However, if your top choice is a private or public university, they may choose instead to contact the highest national university on your list first. It costs MEXT less to place you at a national university than at a public or private one. National universities waive tuition for

MEXT Scholars. At public and private universities, MEXT has to pay your tuition to the university on your behalf.

During the placement process, you may hear unofficial results from your university. For example, your prospective advisor may let you know MEXT has asked them to host you, even though they are not supposed to tell you. If you plan to arrive in April, the university housing office might also contact about spring housing, even though MEXT has not yet announced the formal results. In either of these cases, even if you don't have the formal results, you can treat these unofficial contacts as true.

There is also a possibility that your application could fail at this stage if no university on your Placement Preference Form agrees to accept you. For example, if you did not get any Letters of Provisional Acceptance, MEXT will still contact the universities on your Placement Preference Form to ask them to accept you, but the chances may be lower. If you had submitted at least one Letter of Provisional Acceptance, though, you should be fine!

Once you get the formal results of the Secondary Screening and University Placement from your embassy, then all you have left to do is to pack and prepare for your life in Japan!

Embassy: Competition Level

The Embassy-Recommended MEXT Scholarship competition level is lower than the University-Recommended MEXT Scholarship. It is not *low* by any means! Competition is still intense, so you need to be prepared to work harder than the other applicants.

Each country has a predetermined number of slots available, so you are only competing with other applicants from your country. Sometimes, where there are multiple consulates across the country, the slots available will be further sub-divided among each of the consulates. There is nothing you can do about this. You have to apply at the consulate that serves the area where you live.

In the University-Recommended MEXT Scholarship application process, by comparison, you are competing against all applicants to that university from all countries. The number of slots available will probably be less than the number available to your country through the Embassy-Recommended MEXT Scholarship. That is why I say the competition for the University-Recommended MEXT Scholarship is higher.

If you have multiple nationalities, you do not get to choose where you will apply. You must apply in your "primary" country of citizenship, which is usually the country where you are living at the time of application.

Determining the Number of Available Scholarship Slots

There is no certain list or calculation method, like there is for the University-Recommended MEXT Scholarship, but there are some ways you can make a guess.

Some embassies or consulates might just tell you how many slots they have that year or how many scholarship winners they had the previous year. I have heard from past applicants that they could find out that way. However, they will not tell you how many other applicants there are in total.

Another method is to check the Japanese embassy or consulate's news articles from a year earlier. Depending on how active their PR office is, they might have held an event for all the departing MEXT scholars before they traveled to Japan. If they did, and wrote an article about it, they are likely to list the number of scholars that are going.

Keep in mind that you should search for articles in both spring and fall. The numbers reported in fall may also include scholarship winners through the University-Recommended MEXT Scholarship process.

You can also look for forums, subreddits, or Facebook groups for MEXT scholars. One of the most active forums that I refer to is JREF:

https://mymext.com/jref

When looking for past information, look for information from the 2019/2020 application or later. That was the year that MEXT reduced the number of slots for both the Embassy-Recommended and University-Recommended MEXT Scholarship, so older information may not be accurate.

In almost all cases, the Embassy-Recommended MEXT Scholarship offers a higher number of slots, or at least a higher percentage chance of earning slots, than the University-Recommended MEXT Scholarship. If you are not from a Priority Country (see the list in Appendix C), the Embassy-Recommended MEXT Scholarship might also be your only opportunity to apply!

University-Recommended MEXT Scholarship

The second major application method for the MEXT Scholarship for Research Students is the University-Recommended MEXT Scholarship.

Instead of applying to the Japanese embassy or consulate in your country, you will apply to *one* university in Japan for admission and scholarship nomination all at once. You won't have to go through the embassy at all until after your scholarship is determined and it is time to apply for your visa.

The University-Recommended MEXT Scholarship application process starts later in the year than the Embassy-Recommended MEXT Scholarship. So if you have missed the embassy's deadline, then you will most likely start with this process. You can also apply for the University-Recommended MEXT Scholarship if you learn you have not passed the embassy's primary screening.

Like we did with the Embassy-Recommended MEXT Scholarship, let's look at some advantages and disadvantages of this process first.

Advantages and Disadvantages

The University-Recommended MEXT Scholarship process can be more complicated than the Embassy-Recommended MEXT Scholarship, because each university can start its application process differently, according to its needs. One of the most challenging parts of this process is getting the information specific to the university that you want to apply to.

As a result, not all of the advantages and disadvantages below will apply in each case.

Potential advantages include:

- **Fewer steps:** You don't need to clear both the embassy and university, only the latter. That means you only need to appeal to an academic audience with your proposal.

- **Focus on one university:** In the Embassy-Recommended MEXT Scholarship, you choose up to three universities and professors, which is more effort and can lead to uncertainty in where you will study. In the University-Recommended MEXT Scholarship, you will pursue a single university and single professor from start to finish, allowing for better focus and efficiency.

- **Shorter application process:** The University-Recommended MEXT Scholarship application process begins several months after the Embassy-Recommended MEXT Scholarship, but the scholarship start time is the same. So you will have fewer months of uncertainty between submitting your application and the final results.

- **No local government interference:** Your local government has no say in who gets the scholarship, so if you are concerned about nepotism, discrimination, or corruption, this process is cleaner.

- **PGP programs:** Besides the general category slots, you may be eligible for specific "Priority Graduate Programs", which have a dedicated number of slots with narrow restrictions on applicant eligibility. If you meet the eligibility criteria for one of these programs, your chances of winning the scholarship skyrocket! (more information below)

The key disadvantages to the University-Recommended MEXT Scholarship application process are the cost of applying and the lack of consistent application information:

- **May be restricted to partners:** Some universities in Japan will only accept applications if they have established a formal partnership with your current university.

- **Priority countries:** "General Category" application

slots (non-PGP slots) are only available to applicants from Priority Countries (see Appendix C for details).

- **Application information may be hidden:** Not all universities make it clear how to apply or if they even accept applications. Some universities may select MEXT scholarship candidates out of their pool of general applicants instead of having a separate application process. This means that you would have to apply as a fee-paying applicant in order to become eligible.

- **Test fees:** Unlike the Embassy-Recommended MEXT Scholarship process, you will be required to submit language proficiency test results from internationally accepted tests like TOEFL or IELTS. Some universities may exempt this requirement if your previous degree was taught in English. Some universities may also ask you to submit other test results, such as the GRE.

- **Mailing expenses:** You will have to send application documents by international courier (such as EMS, DHL, etc.) to universities in Japan. If you have to submit replacement documents or correct errors, there's a chance that you'll have to send multiple packages this way.

- **Higher competition:** In almost all cases, competition will be higher for the University-Recommended MEXT

Scholarship, since you'll be competing against applicants from all priority countries, not just your own.

It is possible to mitigate, if not eliminate, most of these disadvantages. If you prepare far enough in advance, you'll have more time to find the application information you need. You might also have a connection with the university that can give you an advantage against the competition, if you reached out during the Embassy-Recommended MEXT Scholarship application period.

Minimizing the cost issue is difficult, but there are two things I can do to help. Part of my goal in this series of books and my website articles is to help you get the application right the first time so that you won't need to resend any documents by courier. I also cover eligibility requirements in the next chapter, so you can be certain in advance that you are eligible and not throwing money away on a lost cause.

I cannot eliminate the costs—you will still have to pay for language tests and some postage—but hopefully I can save you money.

General Category and PGP

In the previous section, I referred to "General Category" and "Priority Graduate Programs (PGP)". Before we go any further, let's get clear on the differences and what that means to you.

General Category

This encompasses almost all the MEXT scholarship slots at universities around Japan. Each university has a designated number of general category slots, based on the number of international graduate students enrolled at the university during the previous year. MEXT allots scholarships per university, not per graduate school, so you will compete with all applicants from all graduate schools for one of the scholarship awards.

We will cover the slot calculation and numbers for some leading universities later in this chapter.

Priority Graduate Programs (PGP)

PGPs are specific degree programs that are pre-selected by MEXT to receive a specific number of scholarship slots each year.

These programs typically have a narrow focus, restricted to one degree level in one graduate school. They might also have other restrictions, such as only being available to applicants from specific nationalities, or only being available to scholars studying in Japanese. Sometimes, that information will not be public.

Each PGP is selected for three years, so if you are applying in 2024, for example, the programs selected in 2022, 2023, and 2024 would still be valid. MEXT finalizes selection of new PGP programs *after* the application deadline at most universities. So you will only be able to see the previous two years' of programs (2022 and 2023 in the example above) when you apply. Universities may launch an additional call for applications for new PGP programs, but it is impossible to know in advance if that will happen.

If you meet the eligibility criteria for one of these programs, your chances of getting the scholarship skyrocket. Instead of competing for a handful of scholarships scattered across the university, you would compete with a much smaller number of students for scholarships designated for your degree program.

Here's one example: When I was processing MEXT scholarship applications for a major university, we received over 200 applications for the University-Recommended MEXT Scholarship one year. We had two PGP programs with 15 combined slots available. Only 16 students met the eligibility requirements for one of those two programs. So, 15 out of those 16 applicants won the scholarship (93.75% success rate). However, only 10 out of the remaining 184 applicants earned a general category scholarship (5.43% success rate). And that was before MEXT cut the General Category slots down to the current maximum of 3 (as of 2024).

I keep updated links to the most recent PGP program lists in my article about How to Apply for the University-Recom-

mended MEXT Scholarship on my website.
https://mymext.com/pgp

(If you signed up for the companion email course for this book, then I will email you to let you know whenever I update that article!)

Unfortunately, these lists will not tell you how many slots each program has or what the eligibility restrictions are, but it will give you a place to look. Research each of the individual programs and universities to see if you can find additional information.

You should not need to do anything extra to designate your application for the PGP program. If you apply to the university and you are eligible for the PGP program, the university would automatically consider your application in that pool. But be sure to check the application guidelines, just in case they have specific instructions.

Other University-Recommended MEXT Scholarship Types

MEXT sometimes allocates additional scholarship slots to universities as part of one of its ongoing initiatives. For example, under the Top Global University initiative that ran from 2014 to 2023, selected universities could nominate up to 10-20 additional students, depending on their TGU grant type. (This was the *total* number of scholarship students, not the number of new nomination per year.) While MEXT's future university grant plans are not clear, similar programs might be available in the future, increasing the number of University-Recommended MEXT Scholarship slots.

Application Timeline

Just like the Embassy-Recommended MEXT Scholarship, I recommend you start preparing your application six months before you plan to apply. If you're applying for both, as I recommend below, this timing should work out well for you. The University-Recommended MEXT Scholarship formal application process begins between September to November, and six months before that is almost exactly the start time of the Embassy-Recommended MEXT Scholarship application process.

If you apply for the Embassy-Recommended MEXT Scholarship and do not pass the primary screening, or if you miss the deadline, prepare your University-Recommended MEXT Scholarship application right away.

The exact application dates are going to vary by university, so be sure you are checking your university's website regularly.

Here's a look at how the application process goes.

1. While preparing your Embassy-Recommended MEXT Scholarship application, determine your field of study

and research question. Start researching and drafting your Field of Study and Research Program Plan (you need to submit this to the embassy, anyway)
When: April-May, 1 year before arrival in Japan
See book 2 of this series: How to Write a Scholarship-Winning Field of Study and Research Program Plan (**https://mymext.com/getmms2**)
*This is not a strict deadline, just a recommendation.

2. Identify your target universities and prospective advisors in Japan. Finish the first draft of your Field of Study and Research Program plan and start reaching out to professors to establish relationships. (Caution: During this time, many other applicants will reach out for Letters of Provisional Acceptance for the Embassy-Recommended MEXT Scholarship, you need to be careful in your communication to avoid confusion).
When: May-July, 1 year before arrival in Japan
See book 3 of this series: How to Find your best Degree Program and Advisor for the MEXT Scholarship (**https://mymext.com/getmms3**) for more details.
*This is not a strict deadline, just a recommendation.

3. Application guidelines released on university websites. Start your application!
When: August-November, 1 year before arrival in Japan
Sometimes, application guidelines may not be re-

leased publicly, so it is important to be in touch with the university.

4. Application submission deadline.
   When: May-June, 1 year before arrival in Japan
   *This is the first real deadline, but the specific date will vary from university-to-university
   MEXT usually releases the new PGP program list in early December, so there may be an addition recruiting period for those programs after than announcement.

5. Application guidelines released on MEXT's website, although it is almost always too late to apply by the time these guidelines are released.
   When: December, 1 year before arrival in Japan

6. Document screening and interviews.
   When: December, 1 year before arrival, to January, year of arrival

7. Universities complete selection, inform candidates, and submit nominations to MEXT.
   When (PGP Programs with April start): Early January, year of arrival
   When (General Category and PGP Programs with Fall Semester Start): January-March, year of arrival
   *PGP candidates nominated by the university are essentially guaranteed to receive the scholarship.

8. Secondary Screening (a.k.a. The Long Wait). MEXT double-checks applications, and makes final confirmation of scholarship awards for all October arrivals.
When (PGP Programs with April start): January-February, year of arrival
When (General Category and PGP Programs with Fall Semester Start): March-July, year of arrival

9. MEXT releases final results to universities and universities contact individual applicants.
When (PGP Programs with April start): February, year of arrival
When (General Category and PGP Programs with Fall Semester Start): June-August, year of arrival (It is supposed to be by the end of June, but MEXT is almost always late).

10. Visa, travel arrangements, and packing for your trip to Japan!
When (PGP Programs with April start): February-March, year of arrival
When (General Category and PGP Programs with Fall Semester Start): July-September, year of arrival

11. Settle in to life in Japan in your degree program or language studies. Establish your day-to-day life and routines. Prepare to extend your scholarship to move on to a degree program if necessary. Start thinking

about inviting your family to join you, if applicable.

When (PGP Programs with April start): April, year of arrival

When (General Category and PGP Programs with Fall Semester Start): September-October, year of arrival

Document Submission and Screening

As I mentioned in the "disadvantages" section earlier, each university has its own application process, to their call for applications and deadlines will vary.

Once you determine the university you want to apply to, research that university and start trying to connect with your desired advisor. (Not as a MEXT applicant at first, but as a student who is genuinely interested in the professor's research. I have more advice on how to contact professors in book 3 of this series.) That is the best way to ensure that you will get the application information you need.

Some universities will only accept applications from students from partner universities, so they will not send out a public call for applications. They will only reach out through their partnerships.

In other cases, universities might not have a separate application process for MEXT scholars. They could select the top candidates each year from their regular, fee-paying applicants. The disadvantage for you in that case is that you would have to pay an application fee. If you win the scholarship, you will get that fee reimbursed later, but if you do not win the scholarship, you would lose that money.

Of course, you could choose to see that as an advantage, too: It will limit the number of applications and therefore the competition.

Even where universities have an open call for applications, the dates can vary. Some schools will close the application deadline in August. Others might not start accepting applications until November.

It is essential that you research your target university in advance!

Researching Your University

Unlike the Embassy-Recommended MEXT Scholarship process, you can only apply to one university per year through this method, so that limits the number of universities you have to research.

The most effective and efficient way to research your target university is through a partnership with your current university. If there is a partnership and you can find a faculty or staff member at your current university that has a connection to the Japanese university, you can inquire through them.

If that is not an option, comb through the Japanese university's website. Look through their news archive to see if they posted an announcement in the previous year to say when MEXT applications were open. Check their admissions pages, particularly the scholarship page for international graduate applicants, if one exists. That is most often where you will find the guidelines. You may even find the previous year's application forms, which will give you an idea of what you need to submit even before they update the page.

Application Forms and Guidelines

You need to get the forms and guidelines from the university, since they can vary.

As you saw in the application timeline earlier, most universities accept applications *before* MEXT releases the official forms for the next year. Because of that time gap, some universities use their own forms or modifications of the forms and ask successful applicants to complete the proper MEXT forms later. You need to be sure that you are following the directions for your university.

If you signed up for my mailing list, I sent you a sample application form. I do not provide blank application forms because they can change from year to year and it is essential that you get the proper form, and any additional required documents, from the university you will apply to.

The guidelines for your university will also tell you when and how to submit your application, so even if the forms are all identical, you'll need to read that document, anyway.

Once you have completed the forms and submitted them, be prepared for a long wait as the university screens applications.

Interviews

MEXT asks all universities to interview applicants during the selection process. These interviews may be in person (unlikely) or conducted by email, Skype, or Zoom. In most cases, the interview will come after the university makes an initial cut based on the documents. If you get an interview request, it's a good sign, but it's not necessarily a guarantee yet.

Unlike the Embassy-Recommended MEXT Scholarship application process interviews, the university is going to focus on the academic side of your goals in the interview. So, while you won't have to deal with bureaucrats and general questions, you will face more intense academic screening because the reviewer will be an expert in your field. You need to be prepared to discuss your Field of Study and Research Program Plan in detail and answer general knowledge questions about your academic field to establish that you are prepared for a graduate degree.

There may still be some questions about your goals or ability to adjust to life in Japan, so do not ignore that preparation, either!

Nomination and MEXT Screening

Once the university has finished its review, they will reach out to let successful candidates know they have been selected for nomination to MEXT.

At this point, you are permitted to celebrate! Except for the budget crisis issue in 2019, every general category and PGP applicant I have ever heard of who was nominated by the university for the scholarship ended up receiving it.

Most universities should also contact waiting list candidates and unsuccessful candidates, as well.

If you are a waiting list candidate, the only way to get elevated to a full candidate is if one of the selected nominees withdraws before the deadline for universities to submit their nominations to MEXT. Unfortunately, that is very unlikely since universities tend to finish their screening right before the nomination deadline. Almost every time I have had a nominee withdraw, it was after the deadline, so it was too late for us to recommend an alternate.

If you are one of the unsuccessful candidates, don't take it too hard. It is probable that only one applicant per field of study earned nomination for the scholarship. You could have been the second-best candidate in all of science and engineering, out of scores of applicants from all over the world, and still miss out.

MEXT Secondary Screening

As with the Embassy-Recommended MEXT Scholarship, this is not a competitive process. MEXT is concerned with double-checking your eligibility, ensuring that you have not applied and been recommended by two different universities, and also checking its own budget.

Japanese universities should all have experience in this application process, so there is no reason to think that there would be a problem with your eligibility after the university's screening.

If you have applied to and earned a scholarship nomination from multiple universities, MEXT will flag that and will disqualify you. It may also choose to disqualify every other applicant from all the universities that recommended you. This should never be a problem, as long as you only applied to one university, but if you find you have earned a nomination from multiple universities, contact all but one of them to withdraw *before* they send your name to MEXT.

The Japanese fiscal year ends in March, between when universities nominate candidates to MEXT and when MEXT makes its final decision. If there is a budget crisis and MEXT has its funding cut, they could choose to award fewer scholarships. However, the only time I saw this happen was in 2019, the year that Japan implemented free university and free kindergarten for low-income families, which required a major budget revision.

University: Competition Level

Competition is going to be higher for the University-Recommended MEXT Scholarship application process. Unless, of course, you qualify for one of the PGP Programs!

Unlike the Embassy-Recommended MEXT Scholarship, it is possible to estimate the number of General Category places available at each university. The number of scholarship slots is based on the number of international graduate students enrolled at that university each year.

MEXT releases a chart every year that shows how many places are available based on the number of enrolled international students. The chart is released along with the University-Recommended MEXT Scholarship application guidelines and forms. As we covered above, this comes after most universities' application deadlines, so the best you can do is refer to the previous year's figures for an estimate. As of the 2023/2024 application cycle, the maximum number of General Category slots was three. Any university with 201 or more international graduate students enrolled qualified for all three slots.

In order to find the number of international graduate students at a university, you can check the university website to see if they publish it. Or you can refer to JASSO's annual report on the number of international students in Japan. While this report is only in Japanese, JASSO reports on the total number of international students in Japan and lists the top universities by international student enrollment. This report shows the *total* number of international students, not just graduate students, so you would need further research or an estimate to determine how many of those students are graduate students.

It's a lot of work. That's the bad news. The good news is that I've already done it for you.

According to JASSO's 2023 Survey (the most recent as of the time of publication), the universities below have at least 1,000 international students enrolled. The same survey shows that graduate students make up 78% of all international students at national universities, 59% at public universities, and 23% at private universities. So you can be reasonably sure that any university with at least 1,000 international students will have at least 201 international students at the graduate level and therefore have three scholarship slots.

List of Universities with over 1,000 International Students enrolled as of May 2023 (alphabetical)

- Doshisha University

- Hiroshima University

- Hokkaido University

- Hosei University

- Japan University of Economics

- Kansai University

- Keio University

- Kobe University

- Kyoto College of Graduate Studies, The

- Kyoto Seika University

- Kyoto University

- Kyushu University

- Meiji University

- Nagoya University

- Nihon University

- Osaka University

- Ritsumeikan Asia Pacific University

- Ritsumeikan University

- Sophia University

- Takushoku University

- Teikyo University

- Tohoku University

- Tokai University

- Tokyo Institute of Technology

- Tokyo International University

- Tokyo University of Social Welfare

- Toyo University

- University of Tokyo, The

- University of Tsukuba

- Waseda University

(JASSO, "Result of International Student Survey in Japan, 2023")

Priority Countries and Slots

MEXT has a list of priority countries (see Appendix C) and requires that 75% of each university's nominees for the General Category and each PGP program come from those countries. Since the maximum number of General Category slots in 2022, that means it is impossible for universities to nominate candidates from non-Priority countries for those slots. The 2023/2024 University-Recommended MEXT Scholarship application guidelines require universities to only nominate Priority Country students for the General Category. Applicants from non-Priority Countries can only apply for PGP programs that have four or more slots available.

Dividing Slots Among Graduate Schools

Keep in mind that those numbers are for the whole university. That means that all applicants in all fields of study will be in competition with one another for slots.

Top Global University Project Universities and Extra Slots

Universities selected for MEXT's "Top Global University Project" had additional MEXT Scholarship slots available. While that program ended in March 2024, it is possible that future MEXT programs will include the same conditions. Slots for these programs follow the rules of the "Domestic Selection" category of MEXT Scholarship slots described below.

Rise to the Competition!

Don't let that discourage you. Let it be motivation. You need to be the best applicant and you can be, if you are willing to put in the effort. Throughout the rest of this book and series, I will share advice from over a decade of working with applicants to help you improve your chances.

Applying to Both: Embassy and University

You can only apply for one application process at a time. But because of the way the application timelines work, you *can* apply to both application processes sequentially, if you have to.

Applying for the Embassy-Recommended MEXT Scholarship First

For the Embassy-Recommended MEXT Scholarship, you need to submit your application documents in late May or early June. By the end of July, you should know the results of the Primary Screening, which is essentially the same as the final results.

If you pass the Primary Screening, then it is almost certain that you will win the scholarship, so there is no reason to apply for the University-Recommended MEXT Scholarship. If you are rejected after the Primary Screening, it would most likely be because of a problem large enough that it would prevent you from receiving the University-Recommended MEXT Scholarship, too. (For example, a record of being deported from Japan in the past, or researching weapons technology.)

If you do not pass the Primary Screening, then you still have time to apply that year for the University-Recommended

MEXT Scholarship between August and December (depending on the university).

In that case, you would not be breaking any rules. Your Embassy-Recommended MEXT Scholarship would be over before the University-Recommended MEXT Scholarship began. Plus, since you would have started your field of study and research program plan and started contacting universities, you should have an advantage over other applicants.

Applying for the University-Recommended MEXT Scholarship First

If you apply for the University-Recommended MEXT Scholarship, you will know between January and March whether the university has decided to nominate you to MEXT for the scholarship. Just like with the Embassy-Recommended MEXT Scholarship, being nominated is practically a guarantee of earning the scholarship. So, in that case, there would be no need for you to apply to the embassy. Instead, you should focus on preparing to move to Japan.

If you do not pass the university's screening, then you have plenty of time to prepare for the Embassy-Recommended MEXT Scholarship application process that will begin in April to June of the next year.

After the Embassy or University nominates you to MEXT, it can be a long wait before you get your final results. I know many applicants get nervous during this time and feel tempted to apply for a back-up option. But as I covered above, MEXT's Secondary Screening is *not* competitive and there should be nothing to worry about. They are just bureaucratic and slow!

If you've got your heart set on the MEXT scholarship and you have no intention of giving up, you can continue this cycle for years. I have known applicants who earned the scholarship in their second or third year of applying. Each time you go through the process, refine your Field of Study and Research Program Plan, and practice the interviews, you become a stronger candidate.

Of course, our goal with these books is to give you the advantage of past applicants' experience so that you can earn the scholarship in your first attempt.

Domestic Selection

Besides the Embassy-Recommended MEXT Scholarship and University-Recommended MEXT Scholarship, there is sometimes a third path to the MEXT scholarship, formerly called Domestic Selection. Until 2023, this was part of the Top Global University program, but since that program is over, it is not clear if it will continue to exist in the future. But I will describe how it works, below.

While the Embassy and University-Recommended MEXT Scholarships are determined before you arrive in Japan, Domestic Selection slots can be used more flexibly. Some universities might make these scholarship slots available to current students who could then start a MEXT Scholarship after arriving in Japan. This was the original intent, hence the name of "Domestic" Selection—for students already studying in Japan. Other universities use it for new students, to supplement the University-Recommended MEXT Scholarship slots.

Difference from the other Scholarship Types

Since the Domestic Selection category was originally for students who are already in Japan, there are some key differences in scholarship benefits and the results timeline.

- **Benefits:** Domestic Selection scholars do not get

their travel to Japan covered by MEXT. This scholarship application process assumes you are already in Japan or that you already intend to travel to Japan on your own to enroll in a university.

- **Selection Timeline:** Expect results from this scholarship type to be released later. For example, for scholarships starting in the fall, results might not come out until August, even though the "normal" University-Recommended MEXT Scholarship results come out in June or July. If others have received their results but you are still waiting, it is possible that you are in this category. The reason for the later selection, again, is that they assume you are already in Japan and don't need to plan a visa application and travel.

Other than those difference, once you start your scholarship, you will receive the same benefits as any other MEXT Scholar. The difference is only up to when you start your studies.

Exercise 1: Determining Your Approach

As promised in the introduction, here is your Chapter One exercise. I recommend following along with these exercises as you go along. By the end of this book, your exercises should provide you with an application plan and an application strategy that will give you an edge over the competition.

You can fill out your answers in a notebook or download the exercise worksheets that go with the book at:

https://mymext.com/bonusmms1

In this first exercise, we're going to establish your application approach.

Your Degree

1. What degree do you want to earn by the end of your scholarship? (Master's / PhD / Professional Master's / Professional Doctorate)

2. What is the first degree you need to earn to get there?

3. Do you have a reason that you need to earn your degree quickly and return to your home country (e.g. if you are on a leave of absence from work)?

4. Are you applying to repeat a degree that you have already earned? If so, why?

Your Application Schedule

5. What month is it as you are reading this?

Ideally, you should start preparing for your application about 2-6 months or more before the application deadline. The deadlines should be around May for the Embassy-Recommended MEXT Scholarship or October for the University-Recommended MEXT Scholarship. You can prepare in less time, but it will require significantly more concentrated work.

6. Based on the explanation above, what application process are you going to apply for first? (Embassy / University)

Your Goals and Resources

7. What is your life goal that will benefits from earning the degree above via the MEXT Scholarship? (It can be a broad goal for now, we will refine it later!)

8. What practical resources do you have that you can use to aid your scholarship application?

- Contact with your academic advisor from your last degree

- Contact with a professor in your field in Japan

- A strong relationship with an academic professional who can review your Field of Study

- Access to a university library

- Contact with someone who has won the scholarship in the past

- Contact with a friend or professional who can proof-read your application

- Other

Chapter Two

Successful Applicant Mindset

S houldn't it be enough just to be an outstanding student with an excellent research plan?

Maybe it should be, but the fact is that it isn't. You might have the best research plan in the world, but if you can't communicate it to the scholarship reviewers, or if you don't meet their expectations for communication and courtesy, then your chances of winning the scholarship will sink faster than a raft in a typhoon.

If you were just trying to get in to a Japanese graduate school, there's a chance that you could do that on the strength of your academic record, alone. But you're applying for the MEXT scholarship. You are competing with the best scholars from around the world to earn one of a few scholarship slots. You need to stand out, and that means taking not only your research, but the application process itself, seriously.

You *can* do this. You can set yourself out from the crowd. All it takes is deliberate focus and a little extra work.

The first thing we're going to cover in this chapter is how you can take a professional approach to the scholarship application. Don't just skip this chapter because it doesn't talk about the practical application forms or where and when to submit your application. We'll cover that later, but your attitude toward the application process comes first.

Your mindset is the most important thing to get in order before you start your application. If you are ready to approach this application with a professional mindset and you understand what you need to do to succeed, then you will set yourself up for success. You will improve the effectiveness of everything else you do. However, if you are not prepared to take the application seriously and are just looking for quick hacks, then no amount of advice I can give will make much of a difference for your chances.

Be Confident

Have any of these questions crossed your mind?

- I don't have any publications. Will I still have a chance?

- I've never been to Japan. Will that put me at a disadvantage?

- I don't have any professional experience, or research experience, etc. Is that going to hurt my application?

- I'm majoring in humanities. Can I even compete with engineering or science majors?

Hundreds of applicants have emailed me with those questions or posted them in the comments on my website over the years. If that's you, then here is your answer:

You have as much of a chance as anyone, because what you did in the past is not as important as what you will do in the future.

The vast majority of applicants I have worked with—including most successful applicants—were applying while they were still students, with no publications, no professional experience, and no previous trips to Japan.

Your experience is valuable if you can leverage it to show the reviewers how it will help you be a better scholar. But even if you don't have the specific experiences I listed above, you surely have some experience you can leverage. We'll cover specific strategies later in chapter 4. For now, the important takeaway is not to let your experience or lack of experience hold you back.

While competition for the MEXT scholarship is high, what will determine your success is how hard you will work to make your application as strong as possible.

Less than 5% of international students in Japan are MEXT scholars. It may seem like you have to get lucky to become one of those few. But as film producer Samuel Goldwyn once said, "The harder I work, the luckier I get."

Decide that you are going to put in the work to earn this scholarship and you can be confident that you have every chance of success.

Be Professional

If you were going to apply for a job that would pay 10,000,000 yen, plus give you the chance to earn a master's degree and PhD for free, how would you approach that application? How much care would you give to the job application form? How would you act in the interview?

We covered the benefits in the previous chapter, so you know the MEXT scholarship can be worth that much, just counting your monthly stipend. Plus, the degrees will continue to pay off for you for the rest of your life, with job opportunities in the future.

So, how would you prepare for that kind of job application?

Surprisingly, a lot of applicants don't take it seriously at all. They are careless or even rude to the reviewers and staff. They are disorganized and appear lazy and whiny.

You want to approach every interaction and every document you submit as if that one thing could make the difference between receiving 10,000,000 yen or not. If you adopt a professional manner, you will be ahead of a significant number of applicants. And the more you take a serious and professional approach to the application, the more likely the embassy and university staff are to treat you the same way.

Here are a few key areas you need to be sure to get right:

Professional Communication and Appearance

I used to get emails like the message below:

————————

"Dear Sensei,

I am an eager and active young student from country X and I want to study at your university with the MEXT scholarship.

I would be honored if you could nominate me for the scholarship.

Looking forward to your urgent reply.

Set from my iPhone"

————————

It almost takes work to be that rude and unprofessional in such a brief email. I have an entire chapter on professional email communication in Book 3 of this series, but here are some problems with this message:

- **Dear Sensei:** The applicant didn't even bother to look up the name and title of the person he was sending to. He sent it to an admin office, so the person reading it wasn't a "sensei", anyway.

- **Multiple Addresses:** You can't tell this from the excerpt above, but I would get emails like this with 10 or more universities in the "To" line of the email, so I could see that the applicant was just sending the same lazy message to as many people as possible. Sending an email to multiple universities in BCC is just as bad.

- **No Knowledge of the University/Professor:** Nothing in this email shows that the applicant has taken the time to research the degrees offered at the university, the research, or the professors. He is just seeking a scholarship and has nothing to offer in return.

- **Urgent Reply:** On top of everything else, the applicant is being demanding of the recipient's time after taking no time to do any work himself.

- **No Name:** Even if your email address is your name (and for many applicants it isn't), it's rude to not write your name in the signature of your message. This is not a text message.

- **Sent from my iPhone:** The applicant didn't even take the time to sit down at a computer and type a proper email. He might have sent this message while he was bored waiting for a bus. While it may be your usual habit to write emails on your phone, in Japan business emails are still treated as letters sent electronically and expected to be formal and well thought-out.

Email etiquette may differ from country to country, but as a professional, it is your responsibility to find out what the expectations are from the perspective of the person on the receiving end and to live up to them. Don't worry, I have you covered!

Presenting a professional appearance in physical interviews—and even when submitting your application documents at the embassy—is equally important. Go in there like you are walking into a corporate job interview worth 10 million yen. (Yes, I keep repeating that number. It's important to remember what's at stake!) This applies to virtual interviews, too!

Professional Preparation

Would you walk into a 10,000,000 yen job interview without having researched the company and its expectations in advance? I hope not. You would know everything there is to know about the company's mission and history. You would know what they are looking for in an employee, and you would know what questions they are likely to ask and how you plan to respond.

You would also know which of your strengths you need to emphasize to give you the best chance at getting the job.

Approach the scholarship in the same way. Taking the application seriously means knowing what MEXT wants out of its scholarship recipients the goals and desired outcomes of the scholarship program from MEXT's perspective. It means knowing what the universities and your potential advisor wants out of its students. And it means being prepared to address those questions in every document and interview.

We will cover this more in Chapter 4, about your application strategy, later in this book. In later books, we will come back to this as you write your Field of Study and Research Program Plan and contact potential advisors, too.

Timeliness

Timeliness is the cornerstone of professionalism. You already know that turning in an assignment late at university can cause reduced points or zero credit. In the professional world, timeliness is more important. If you cannot deliver goods and services on time, you can lose contracts or lose your job.

In Japan, timeliness is sacred.

In 2017, an incident made international news when a Japanese train departed the station 20 seconds early. The company apologized profusely for the error, which was abnormal and unacceptable in Japan. However, what made the story international news was the comparison between the Japanese system and the rest of the world. News media in other countries expressed shock that 20 seconds was such a big deal. In Japan, it absolutely is.

When we accepted scholarship applications in person at my university in Japan, the submission deadline was 17:00:00, according to our atomic clock. We had staff standing by at the door as the time approached and as soon as the clock ticked over to the hour, we would lock it, even a student was running toward the door and three steps away. We never accepted any excuses.

As you go through this application process, do not procrastinate. If the embassy or university contacts you, you should be prepared to reply within 24 hours. And not from a smartphone, like in the message above. Even if you can't answer their question or submit the document they requested within that 24-hour window, it is polite to reply to acknowledge the message, tell them you are working on it, and let them know when you will submit it.

On the other hand, do not hold the university or embassy to the same expectations. The embassy and university are the ones who get to decide who earns the scholarship. They do not have to be as polite to you as you have to be to them. Sure, in an ideal world, they would be. But understand, too, that you are one of hundreds of applicants they are dealing with at once, and they can't get back to everyone as quickly as they want to.

Even though it might grate on you to have to wait, part of being professional means understanding their situation and respecting their time. And of course, knowing when it is time to send a polite reminder, as well.

A professional mindset is a minimum requirement to succeed in the MEXT scholarship application. Approach this scholarship with the same mindset that you would take for a 10,000,000 yen job application and you will already be at an advantage over a significant number of applicants!

Don't Be Arrogant

The single greatest failure I have seen among applicants—the reason most eliminated themselves from competition—is thinking only about themselves.

The last step we're going to cover in your mindset is to grasp the bigger picture. You need to think about the other applicants (your competition) and what they are doing. You need to think about each person who you talk to during the application process and what their perspective is. Understanding your place in the greater system is going to help you get much closer to success.

Think About Other Applicants

The competition level for the MEXT scholarship is high. Expect to have at least 20 applicants for every scholarship slot available.

I don't want you to let this get you down. I want you to use it as motivation. Whenever you're thinking about cutting corners, or considering a document "good enough", ask yourself in your competition will be trying harder. Think about how much extra effort you need to put in to beat out the other applicants and make sure you aren't eliminating yourself by giving up too easily.

Think About the Reviewers

Almost everyone you interact with during the application process is looking for reasons to eliminate applicants in order to narrow down the selection pool. Make sure you leave them with the impression that you are one that they want to keep around.

Because of the competition numbers I mentioned above, the reviewers at the embassy and even at the university cannot hope to give every application the attention that it deserves. They have to narrow down the applicants to those who have the most promise as quickly and efficiently as possible. Even then, they cannot give every applicant and application the attention you think you deserve.

Throughout the application process, but especially at the early stages, understand that you are not going to get the personal attention you want. To the reviewers at this stage, you are just one of a sea of applicants and they may well operate by the standard Japanese rule of fairness:

If they cannot offer something to all applicants at once, they will not offer it to any at all.

Here are some examples of how applicants can go wrong in their relationship building with the reviewers, and what you can do to avoid the mistakes.

How to Kill Your Application Chances

- **Applying when not eligible:** Obviously, this is the first elimination criteria. In the next chapter in this book, we'll walk through your eligibility criteria together so you can be sure this won't be a problem for you.

- **Unprofessional or careless communication:** We covered this above and will go into detail in Book 3 of this series when we discuss reaching out to your prospective advisor. In my experience, this is a particular problem in email communications with your university. Careless writing in an email can lead to miscommunication between two people who share a common first language and cultural background, and the risks are much greater when you don't even have that advantage. Re-read your email before you send it to make sure there are no areas where you are inviting misunderstanding.

- **Asking questions you should be able to find the answers to yourself:** Some people never bother to do any research on their own and skip straight to asking questions. I see this all the time on my website and in handling emails from students at work. Don't jump straight to sending a question by email until you have reviewed the embassy or university's website and made sure that the answer is not already there. Otherwise, you risk showing them you are too lazy or incompetent to do basic research on your own. And when you *do* write an email (because there will be some things that are unclear in their instructions, I guarantee it), be sure to show that you have researched the question as best as possible on your own, but could not find the answer. Remember, you are applying to be a *research* student. The embassy and university staff will expect you to show the initiative to find information on your own. Since you have invested in yourself with a book on the application process, I think you are prepared to do what it takes to improve your application, but make sure that you carry that mindset forward in your interaction with the embassy and university.

- **Asking for exceptions:** Applicants used to email me all the time to ask for exceptions to the application requirements or to the application process. My answer was no. It had to be, unless there was a specific alternative pre-approved. For one thing, MEXT sets the requirements and nobody at the university had the authority to override them. And for another, I had 200 applicants who *were* willing and able to meet the requirements. Do not ask for exceptions or exemptions if you can avoid it. And if you do, make sure you provide a clear reason the situation is beyond your control (for example, if your recommender insists on sending the letter to the embassy/university) or why it is worth the university or embassy's time and effort to consider you for special treatment. If you must ask for an exception, provide the embassy or university with an alternative that is easy and convenient for them to accept.

- **Tardiness:** We covered this in the section on being professional, so I won't spend too much time on it. One of the easiest way to get yourself eliminated is to miss a deadline. Keep in mind that most Japanese deadlines are "arrive by" deadlines, not postmark deadlines. If something is due by mail, then it must be in the university's hands by 17:00 on the deadline day, not just in the mail. Also, keep the time difference in mind! If you are communicating with the university, their time zone is ahead of yours and they will consider the cut-off time and date according to their clock, not yours. Submit early to avoid any deadline misses. "My internet crashed right before the deadline" is never acceptable as an excuse.

Remember the numbers. Think about the competition and the sheer volume of applicants that the university and embassy have to deal with. If you are ever in doubt, ask yourself if your action is going to put you ahead of or behind your competition. If you think about the bigger picture in this way, act professional, and maintain the confidence that you can win this scholarship, you should be set up for success!

Now that we have your mindset in order, let's go cover that first item on the list: making sure you are eligible to apply.

Exercise 2: Mindset

Let's stop now and make sure you have your mindset right. We will not go into too much detail, because we'll save that for the chapter on your application strategy later. For now, I just want to know that you're with me. I believe you can do this. I want to make sure you believe it, too, and that you're willing to do what it takes to make this work.

As before, you can fill out your answers in a notebook or download the exercise worksheets that go with the book at:

https://mymext.com/bonusmms1

OK, let's get started.

Confidence

This is an exercise I still use every time I think I don't have what it takes. It always helps me at least to pretend that I have the confidence I need long enough to get the job done.

1. Are you concerned you won't be able to compete for the MEXT scholarship?

2. Why? What disadvantages do you think you have? Be specific.

3. Do you think no other applicant has those same problems or concerns?

4. If every other applicant is human, too, with strengths and weaknesses, what strengths do you have that can set you apart from them? (Here's one: You're a person who invested the time and money in yourself to succeed, as evidenced because you're reading this book and following through with the exercises!)

5. If you apply for the scholarship and don't get it, what's the worst that could happen to you? Again, be specific.

6. So what? Is that worse than what happens if you never apply at all?

Professionalism

7. Imagine *you* were offering an award worth 10,000,000 yen. How would you expect applicants to address you in an email?

8. What characteristics would you look for in their plans?

9. How would you expect applicants to dress and prepare mentally for an interview?

10. On a more practical matter, how often do you check your email and what alerts and systems can you set up to make sure you notice important messages?

Humility

11. Do you think you need any special consideration during the application process? (e.g. no language proficiency scores, financial difficulty in sending materials or traveling to the embassy)

12. What can you do on your own to overcome those challenges?

13. Do you communicate well in writing in English?

14. Is there someone you could ask to test your emails to the embassy and university to make sure your message gets across? Preferably, choose someone who is timely, reliable, and not afraid to give you their frank opinion.

15. Do you immediately asks questions or do you do research on your own? If you tend to ask questions before doing your own searching, what can you do to help yourself overcome that problem?

Chapter Three

Eligibility

You must be eligible to apply.

While there are some exceptions built into the rules, there is no possibility of obtaining a personal exception to the eligibility criteria otherwise. So, you cannot apply if you don't meet the requirements we'll discuss in this chapter.

If that's the case for you, I'm sorry. But at least by finding out at this stage, you can save yourself considerable time and money on the application process and focus your efforts on another goal.

The MEXT scholarship eligibility criteria can be confusing. Some criteria, such as the minimum GPA and priority country nationality for the University-Recommended MEXT Scholarship, are only explained to universities as *nomination* criteria to MEXT and do not appear in the application guidelines. Some criteria don't seem to have any objective measurement. In this chapter, I will explain each criterion to make them clear. I will start with the eligibility criteria as written in the application guidelines, then explain what it means to you.

The eligibility criteria below are based on the most recent requirements as of the time of publishing: the 2023/2024 Embassy-Recommended and University-Recommended MEXT Scholarship.

A Note About Language and Translation

For the Embassy-Recommended MEXT Scholarship application process, MEXT publishes the application guidelines, including the eligibility requirements, in English, so I will use their wording (grammatical errors and all). For the University-Recommended MEXT Scholarship application process, MEXT publishes the PGP Category guidelines in English but only publishes the General Category guidelines in Japanese. Where no official English version exists, I will provide my translation and let you know when I do so.

Order of Eligibility Criteria

Instead of following the order in MEXT's guidelines, I will group the eligibility criteria by similar types and address them in order from easiest to most difficult to assess. This may jump around a bit compared to the order in the actual application guidelines, but I will cover everything.

Academic Background and Degree Completion

The Requirement

This is one section where the Embassy and University processes differ.

Embassy-Recommended MEXT Scholarship:

Academic Background: Applicants must satisfy any one of the following conditions for admission to either a master's or doctoral course at a Japanese graduate school in which they wish to first enroll. (Applicants who will certainly satisfy any of the following conditions by the time of enrollment are eligible.)

(a) Master's course / Doctoral course (first phase)

1. Applicants who have completed 16 years of school education in countries other than Japan.

2. Applicants who have completed a program with the standard study period of three years or more at universities or equivalent educational institutions in countries other than Japan and received a degree equivalent to a bachelor's degree.

3. Other than the above 1 and 2 conditions, applicants who are eligible for enrollment in a master's course /doctoral course (first phase) at a Japanese graduate school.

(b) Doctoral course (second phase)

1. Applicants who have been awarded with an overseas degree equivalent to a master's degree or professional degree.

2. Applicants who have graduated from universities and have been involved in research study at universities or research centers (including overseas universities and research centers) for two years or more, and recognized as having academic competency equivalent to persons with a master's degree by the graduate school.

3. Other than the above 1 and 2 conditions, applicants who are eligible for enrollment in a doctoral course (second phase) at a Japanese graduate school.

(c) Doctoral course (faculties of medicine, dentistry, veterinary sciences and certain parts in pharmaceutical fields)

1. Applicants who have completed 18 years of school education in countries other than Japan.

2. Applicants who have completed a program with the standard study period of five years or more at universities or equivalent educational institutions

in countries other than Japan and received a degree equivalent to a bachelor's degree.

3. Applicants who have completed 16 years of school education in countries other than Japan and have been involved in research study at universities or research centers (including overseas universities and research centers) for two years or more, and recognized as having academic competency equivalent to university graduates in medicine, dentistry, veterinary sciences or certain parts in pharmaceutical fields by the graduate school.

4. Other than the above 1, 2 and 3 conditions, applicants who are eligible for enrollment in a doctoral course (faculties of medicine, dentistry, veterinary sciences and certain parts in pharmaceutical fields) at a Japanese graduate school.

※ For (c) above, you must confirm necessary academic background details on the websites of the universities in which you wish to enroll since the academic background needed for admission may vary according to university. [For example, (c)-1 stipulates that applicants must graduate from an undergraduate program in medicine, dentistry, veterinary or pharmaceutical sciences.]

University-Recommended MEXT Scholarship:

> Applicants must satisfy the conditions for admission to either a master's or doctoral course at a Japanese graduate school. (Applicants who will certainly satisfy them at the time of enrollment are eligible.)

Yes, the requirements for the University-Recommended MEXT Scholarship are *much* simpler. MEXT assumes that the university wouldn't nominate you if you weren't qualified.

Interpreting the Requirement

The basic rule of thumb for your academic background is that you must meet all the requirements necessary to enroll in the same level degree program at a university in your home country.

If you are applying for the University-Recommended MEXT Scholarship, the process is straightforward. If the university determines that your academic background is sufficient, that is all you need. Most times, that means that if you're applying for a master's degree, you need to have finished your bachelor's degree (or expect to finish it before arriving in Japan). If you're applying for a doctoral degree, then you would have to have finished or expect to finish your master's degree first. The university would make any case-by-case decision for complicated situations.

If you are applying for the Embassy-Recommended MEXT Scholarship, then the most relevant requirements are number 2 for master's degree applicants and number 1 for doctoral degree applicants. Those requirements state you are eligible if you have completed—or expect to complete—a degree equivalent to a bachelor's degree (for master's applicants) or master's degree (for doctoral applicants) overseas. Remember, a professional degree is a non-academic degree, such as an MBA that is at the master's level.

When MEXT says "expected to complete", it means that you will are still enrolled now, but will complete all requirements for your current degree before you come to Japan. That means that it is possible to apply before you graduate.

If you are applying for medical, dental, pharmaceutical, or veterinary programs, you would need to meet the specific requirements of the universities you intend to apply to in advance, regardless of whether you plan to apply for Embassy or University-Recommended MEXT Scholarship. Education in these fields in Japan comprises a 6-year bachelor's degree followed by a 3- or 4-year doctorate.

Since these programs require you to pass a grueling national professional license exam in Japanese in order to take part in the practical training program, assume that most of these programs, particularly in medicine, will require native-level Japanese language fluency.

Doctoral Program Phases

In the eligibility criteria above, you will see a reference to the first phase and second phase of a doctoral program. There are different words in Japanese for a terminal master's degree (studies that end at a master's degree with no doctoral degree offered at that institution) and studies that offer the possibility of continuing on to a doctoral degree. Most times in English, both translate to "master's degree".

Whenever you see "doctoral degree (first phase)", it means "master's degree" and "doctoral degree (second phase)" means "doctoral degree". Note that admission to the first phase does not guarantee admission to the second. If you intend to continue from a master's degree into a doctoral degree, you would need to apply for admission and apply to extend your MEXT Scholarship.

Basic Eligibility Criteria: Measurable

There are a few basic, measurable eligibility requirements that are quick and easy to check off, so let's cover those first.

Nationality

The Requirement

The requirement for the Embassy-Recommended MEXT Scholarship and University-Recommended MEXT Scholarship is almost identical:

> Applicants must have the nationality of a country that has diplomatic relations with Japan. An applicant who has Japanese nationality at the time of application is not eligible. However, persons with dual nationality who hold Japanese nationality and whose place of residence at the time of application is outside of Japan are eligible to apply as long as they choose the nationality of the other country and renounce their Japanese nationality by the date of their arrival in Japan (the acquisition of student status). The First Screening must be conducted at the Japanese diplomatic mission in

the country of which the applicant chooses the nationality.

The only difference between the two versions is the last sentence above. For the University-Recommended MEXT Scholarship, the university, not the Japanese diplomatic mission, conducts applicant screening.

Note that while it is not stated in the eligibility requirements, applicants for General Category scholarship slots through the University-Recommended MEXT Scholarship must have the nationality of a Priority Country. I have included a list of Priority Countries as of 2023/2024 in Appendix C.

Interpreting the Requirement

Japan recognizes and has diplomatic relations with almost all recognized, independent states. It does not have formal diplomatic relations with Taiwan, North Korea, or disputed states such as South Ossetia, etc., so applicants with those nationalities cannot apply. (For Taiwan, however, there is an independent organization that offers an identical scholarship).

To determine whether Japan has diplomatic relations with your country, the best approach is to search the Ministry of Foreign Affairs' list of Japanese diplomatic missions abroad:

https://mymext.com/embassies

I recommend using the search (Control-F) function on that page, since Japan might not list your country under the region/continent that you are used to. For example, you'll find Mexico in the column for Latin America and the Caribbean, not North America.

Sometimes, Japan may have formal diplomatic relations with your country, but may not have a physical embassy or consulate in your country (or may have moved out of your country because of war, etc.). In that case, there will still be a link on the page above for your country and that will tell you where the Japanese embassy to your country is located. For example, the "Japanese Embassy in Yemen" moved to Riyadh, Saudi Arabia, in 2015. Applicants from Yemen are still eligible, but would apply via the embassy in Riyadh for the scholarship.

Japanese Dual Nationality

If you have dual nationality, including Japanese nationality, you are not eligible to apply unless you renounce your Japanese nationality. Of course, once you pass the age of 20, Japan "requires" you to choose to renounce either your Japanese or foreign nationality, so in theory you would have already had to make that choice. However, there is no enforcement method other than things like this scholarship application process.

Renouncing Japanese nationality is a much larger decision and process than just applying for a scholarship. If you are in that situation, I would recommend that you think about the future costs and benefits and proceed with caution. It probably is not worth it just for the sake of this scholarship.

Age

The Requirement

The requirement for the Embassy-Recommended MEXT Scholarship and University-Recommended MEXT Scholarship is almost identical:

Embassy-Recommended MEXT Scholarship:

> Applicants, in principle, must have been born on or after April 2, 1989*. Exceptions are limited to cases in which MEXT deems that the applicant could not apply within the eligible age limit due to the situation or circumstances of the applicant's country (military service obligation, loss of educational opportunities due to disturbances of war, etc.) Personal circumstances (financial situation, family circumstances, state of health, circumstances related to applicant's university or

place of employment, etc.) will not be considered for exceptions.

University-Recommended MEXT Scholarship:

Applicants, in principle, must be born on or before April 2, 1989.* Exceptions are limited to cases in which MEXT deems that the applicant could not apply within the eligible age limit due to the situation or circumstances of the applicant's country (military service obligation, loss of educational opportunities due to disturbances of war, etc.) Personal circumstances (financial situation, family circumstances, state of health, circumstances related to applicant's university or place of employment, etc.) will not be considered for exceptions.

However, for the Young Leader's Program graduates who do not meet the above age requirements and wish to enroll in a doctoral course, they can apply only within five years after they have completed the program.

*1989 is the year stated in the 2023/2024 application guidelines. The specific year changes with each application cycle and is always 35 years before the year that the scholarship starts.

The only difference between the two criteria above is the exception for graduates of the Young Leaders Program, which only exists for the University-Recommended MEXT Scholarship.

Interpreting the Requirement

It is almost certain that the exceptions do not apply to you. So, all you need to do is calculate your age.

As I mentioned above, you must be born no later than April 2 of the year 35 years before the year you will start your studies in Japan. The numbers above are from the application process for scholars who will arrive in 2024. To find the correct year for your application, subtract 35 from the year you will *arrive in Japan*. The year that you will arrive in Japan is one year later than the year you are applying.

For example, if you are applying in 2024 and will start your studies in 2025, you would have to be born no later than April 2, 1990 (2025 - 35 = 1990).

Note that even if you plan to arrive in Japan in the fall semester, the "April 2" requirement does not change. It is based on the official start of the Japanese fiscal/academic year.

Health

The Requirement

The requirements for the Embassy-Recommended MEXT Scholarship and University-Recommended MEXT Scholarship have different wording but the same meaning:

Embassy-Recommended MEXT Scholarship:

> Applicants must submit a health certificate in the prescribed format signed by a physician attesting that the applicant has no physical or mental conditions hindering the applicant's study in Japan.

University-Recommended MEXT Scholarship:

> Applicants who are judged by the university to have no physical or mental conditions hindering the applicant's study in Japan.

The primary difference here is that there is a required Certificate of Health format for the Embassy-Recommended MEXT Scholarship. MEXT does not require a specific form for the University-Recommended MEXT Scholarship, leaving it up to each individual university to decide. Many universities will use the Embassy-Recommended MEXT Scholarship format, anyway.

Interpreting the Requirement

You must have a physician's certification that you do not require any ongoing care that would make it impossible for you to study in Japan.

I have never seen or heard of a student getting eliminated over this requirement. (However, I once had a student who forged the Certificate of Health because he didn't want to pay a doctor for the exam. That student was disqualified).

The only situations this might apply to are ongoing recovery from a serious disease or injury that requires hospitalization, regular care and therapy that would be impossible in Japan, and/or would prevent you from flying. However, since the application process is several months long, the chances are good that you would have time to complete your care in the meantime, if it was not a chronic condition.

If you have an ongoing condition that you can manage on your own without regular care from the same physician, that should not be a problem. Even where you need regular check-ups, but any doctor in the field could do it (for example, regular blood tests), that would not be an obstacle to studying in Japan. It may be a challenge to you, as finding medical personnel that can give care in English can be challenging in some parts of the country, but it would not affect your eligibility.

Prescription medication would also not affect your eligibility, but you would must secure it from your home country prior to departure and may have to plan regular trips back to your home country for prescription refills if your medication is not available in Japan and cannot be sent through the mail. This may apply in cases of narcotic medicines or other controlled substances. That would not affect your eligibility, it is just something to prepare for.

Language Ability (University-Recommended MEXT Scholarship)

The Requirement

Only the University-Recommended MEXT Scholarship has a specific, measurable requirement. I cover the Embassy-Recommended MEXT Scholarship requirement later in the list of unmeasurable eligibility requirements.

> Applicants must satisfy any one of the following conditions to prove that they have sufficient Japanese or English language ability.

Japanese

1. Applicants must pass with N2 or higher in the Japanese Language Proficiency Test (JLPT) at the time of application.

2. Applicants must complete curriculums that meet the conditions for admission to master's or doctoral courses at Japanese graduate schools using Japanese as the main language.

3. Applicants are regarded by the accepting universities as having Japanese language ability equivalent to or better than 1.

English

1. Applicants must pass or achieve scores in English language proficiency tests that correspond to B2 or higher level in the Common European Framework of Reference for Languages (CEFR) at the time of application.

2. Applicants must complete school curriculums that meet the conditions for admission in masters' or doctoral courses at a Japanese graduate school by using English as the main language.

3. Applicants are regarded by the accepting universities as having English language ability equivalent to or better than 1.

*Please note that applicants nominated as either degree-seeking students or non-regular students must meet requirement 1, 2, or 3 above

for English or Japanese at the time of nomination. Non-regular students who are accepted while meeting requirement 3 are required to meet criteria 1 in English or Japanese at the time of applying to extend their scholarship to become degree-seeking students, so universities must inform students selected as non-regular students of this requirement. Criteria 3 will not be accepted for the scholarship extension application.
*Degree-seeking and non-regular students who are studying in a program that meets the requirements of 2 above at the time of application and who will complete/graduate from that program before enrolling in the university are considered to meet criteria 2.

The notes with asterisks appear only in the Japanese version and are my translation.

Interpreting the Requirement

That is a long requirement to break down. Let's get the simplest parts out of the way first.

Criteria 2 for both languages requires that you complete your qualifying degree with English or Japanese as the "main language" of instruction for that degree. "Main language" means the language of instruction for your content courses.

If you took language courses as part of your degree and those were taught in the target language, that will not hurt you. If the language of instruction for most of your content questions was not English, but you had a few English-taught classes, that would not qualify.

Your qualifying degree, the "curriculum that meets the condition for admissions" is the prerequisite degree to the degree you are applying for in Japan. For example, if you are applying for a master's degree, then the language of your bachelor's degree matters. If you are applying to a doctorate, then the language of instruction for your master's degree is the one that matters. (In that case, the language of instruction for your bachelor's degree does not matter.) If you have multiple degrees at the previous level, then if at least one of them meets the requirement, that is fine.

As shown in the notes, if you are enrolled in a degree that meets the requirements and will graduate before starting your MEXT Scholarship, that counts.

For criteria 1 in Japanese, the requirement is very simple, too: Pass the Japanese Language Proficiency Test (JLPT) level N2.

For criteria 1 in English, while the guidelines do not give an exact measurement, MEXT has provided other documentation that does. In 2017, they developed a chart of scores on the Cambridge assessments, Eiken, GTEC, IELTS, TEAP, TEAP CBT, and TOEFL iBT that fall into each of the CEFR ranges.

The chart is still available on the MEXT website as of this publication.

Test Name	Minimum B2 Equivalent Score	Notes
Cambridge Assessments	160	There are multiple tests in the Cambridge Assessments. This score can be earned in the Cambridge Preliminary, First, and Advanced. The minimum possible score on the Cambridge Proficiency is 180 (higher than B2)
Eiken	2300	There are multiple levels to the Eiken. This score can be earned on the Pre-Level 1 (although the minimum passing score is 2304) and the Level 1 (minimum possible score is 2304).
GTEC	1190	There are multiple tests in the GTEC series. This score can be earned on the Advanced and CBT tests.
IELTS	5.5	
TEAP	309	
TEAP CBT	600	
TOEFL iBT	72	

Make sure that your test scores are official! Your university or language schools in your city may offer prediction tests, equivalency tests, or institutional tests for much lower cost, but do not expect that universities will accept them. Official tests are more expensive, but the MEXT scholarship is a merit-based scholarship, not a need-based scholarship. Arguments that you can't afford the test will not get you any traction.

Individual universities may accept other tests that have been mapped to the CEFR by verified research at their discretion. Check the universities' websites to see which tests they accept.

Finding Testing Centers and Dates

Of the test above, IELTS and TOEFL are the most common worldwide. The links below should help you identify the next available tests in your area for those and for the JLPT.

- TOEFL iBT Online Portal:
  https://mymext.com/toefl

- IELTS Test Dates and Locations:
  https://mymext.com/ielts

- JLPT Test Dates and Locations:
  https://mymext.com/jlpt

I haven't mentioned criteria 3 because I have never seen an example of it. The only situation I can imagine would be if the university already knew you and your English or Japanese language ability, personally, such as from an exchange program or joint project, but you had no test score at the time of the application. Even that is so rare of a possibility that it isn't worth mentioning. Don't put your hopes in criteria 3.

Basic Eligibility Criteria: Unmeasurable

Besides the measurable criteria, there are some "eligibility criteria" that have no objective measurement.

While there is no specific standard to meet here, you should know these criteria, as you may get asked about them during the application or interview process. Depending on your answer, they could get you eliminated, if the reviewer gets the wrong impression from you.

Language Ability (Embassy-Recommended MEXT Scholarship)

We covered the language proficiency requirement for the University-Recommended MEXT Scholarship above. The Embassy-Recommended MEXT Scholarship does not have a similar, measurable language proficiency requirement and does not require applicants to submit language proficiency test scores. Instead, all applicants who pass the document screening take language proficiency tests during the Primary Screening process at the embassy. So, the "eligibility requirement" for the Embassy-Recommended MEXT Scholarship is quite simple.

The Requirement

Applicants must be willing to learn Japanese. Applicants must be interested in Japan and be willing to deepen their understanding of Japan after arriving in Japan. Applicants must also have the ability to do research and adapt to living in Japan.

Interpreting the Requirement

The eligibility requirement for the embassy is unmeasurable. There is no objective way to tell if you are "willing to learn Japanese" or "interested in Japan". This requirement makes sure that you want to study in Japan and aren't just applying because it's a generous scholarship.

The application form for the Embassy-Recommended MEXT Scholarship includes the essay questions, "What was your trigger for having an interest in Japan?" and "Why did you choose Japan as a destination to study graduate-level education?" Valid answer to those questions, especially if related to your research and language interest, should clear this requirement.

Language ability also comes into play in the "Field of Study" eligibility criteria that we will discuss a little later.

It is important to note that if you're applying by Embassy-Recommended MEXT Scholarship, you also have to meet the universities' requirements when you apply for a Letter of Acceptance later. While this is not a matter of "eligibility", just be aware that you may need language proficiency test scores, after all, if your university demands them. It's always better to have them than not.

Willingness to Get Involved

The Requirement

The requirement for the Embassy-Recommended MEXT Scholarship and University-Recommended MEXT Scholarship is identical:

> MEXT Scholarship will be granted those who are willing to contribute to mutual understanding between Japan and their home country by participating in activities at schools and communities during their study in Japan while contributing to the internationalization of Japan. They shall also make efforts to promote relations between the home country and Japan by maintaining close relations with the university attended after graduation, cooperating with the conducting of sur-

veys and questionnaires, and cooperating with relevant projects and events conducted by Japanese diplomatic missions after they return to their home countries.

Interpreting the Requirement

While this is not measurable, you can address it in your Field of Study and Research Program Plan, in your interview, and in the essay questions for the Embassy-Recommended MEXT Scholarship.

When writing the research timeline portion of the Field of Study and Research Program Plan, particularly for the University-Recommended MEXT Scholarship, where other opportunities are scarce, include a reference to finding local community activities to get involved in. If you can relate these activities to your research field, such as presenting your research to relevant communities in Japan or giving related lessons to community groups, that is a great thing to identify. But even if your research does not relate to community interaction, it is still beneficial to clarify that you plan to proactively seek opportunities to contribute to the community while in Japan. Specific references are always better.

In the Embassy-Recommended MEXT Scholarship application form, there is an essay question that asks, "What kinds of things do you think you can contribute to Japan and your home country through your experience of studying in Japan?" Your answer to that question should clarify that you meet this eligibility requirement!

If you mention your willingness to get involved in your Field of Study or Research Program Plan or in your interview, keep it brief and stay focused on your research. All you need to do is "check the box". Do not waste space or time going into detail.

Arrival in Japan

The Requirement

The requirement for the Embassy-Recommended MEXT Scholarship and University-Recommended MEXT Scholarship (PGP) is identical other that the first paragraph, in brackets below:

> [Applicants must choose and fill in the Application Form either of the following arrival periods 1 or 2. In principle, a change in the arrival period is not permitted after the submission of the Application Form.]
>
> 1. April term: In principle, applicants must be able to arrive in Japan between April 1, 2024, and

April 7, 2024. Departure from the home residence should be on or after April 1, 2024.

2. October term: In principle, applicants must be able to arrive in Japan during the period specified by the accepting university within two weeks before and after the starting date of the university's relevant academic term (September or October) for that year. Excluding cases in which MEXT deems as unavoidable circumstances, the applicant must withdraw from this scholarship program if the applicant cannot arrive in Japan by the end of the specified period above which decided by MEXT or the accepting university.

2024 is the year stated in the 2023/2024 application guidelines. The specific year changes with each application cycle.

The requirement for the University-Recommended MEXT Scholarship (General category) is the same as item 2 from the example above:

In principle, applicants must be able to arrive in Japan during the period specified by the accepting university within two weeks before and after the starting date of the university's relevant academic term (September or October) for that year. Excluding cases in which MEXT deems as unavoidable circumstances, the applicant must withdraw from this scholarship program if the applicant cannot arrive in Japan by the end of the specified period above which decided by MEXT or the accepting university.

Interpreting the Requirement

This requirement is unmeasurable at the time of application. That might be why it shows up again later in the disqualification criteria.

The minor differences in the wording are based on the programs. For the Embassy-Recommended MEXT Scholarship, you get to choose whether you want to arrive in Japan for the April term or October term. For the University-Recommended MEXT Scholarship, you do not get a choice. General category scholarships start only in the October term. PGP programs are designated as April-start or October-start, depending on the program.

The exception mentioned here dates from the COVID-19 pandemic and closing of Japan's borders. Since borders have reopened, don't expect MEXT to approve any other "unavoidable circumstances" for anything less than a similar disaster.

You cannot choose to delay your arrival or defer your scholarship award for any reason.

There are two things you need to consider here:

1. There must be nothing in your home country that would prevent you from leaving on schedule, and

2. There must be no reason you would be ineligible to enter Japan.

If you are working, you will have to be able to leave your job and arrive in Japan by the date specified by MEXT and the university. You cannot change your arrival dates because of work or personal circumstances.

The same goes if you are still in school. If there is some last event you want to attend at your previous university, such as a degree conferment ceremony, you could not delay your trip to Japan for that.

One other precaution to look out for here is that there are some countries that do not allow their citizens (or government employees) free access to their own passports. If you need permission from your home country's government to get your passport and leave the country, secure that in advance.

Regarding entering Japan, if you have been deported from Japan in the past or departed under a Departure Order, there is a specific period during which you may not reenter the country. You are not eligible to apply for the MEXT scholarship if it would mean entering Japan again during that period. But, hopefully, that does not apply to you!

Disqualification Criteria

There are several disqualification criteria that will eliminate you from the application process and can result in cancelation of your scholarship if discovered after you arrive in Japan.

If your scholarship is canceled after arriving in Japan because you are found to meet one of the disqualification criteria, it would be canceled under the condition of "voluntary withdrawal" from the scholarship. In that case, you would not need to pay back any scholarship amount awarded.

These criteria are straightforward and easy to identify, so you do not need to worry about tricky definitions or gray areas. We'll go through them once now so you can ensure you meet all the requirements and have nothing to worry about.

For all other eligibility requirements we cover, you must meet the criteria described to be eligible. However, for the disqualification criteria, the MEXT guidelines write them in a way that anyone who meets the description is *ineligible*.

Military Affiliation

The Requirement

The requirement for the Embassy-Recommended MEXT Scholarship and University-Recommended MEXT Scholarship is identical:

> Those who are military personnel or military civilian employees at the time of their arrival in Japan or during the period of the payment of the scholarship.

Interpreting the Requirement

As long as you are not employed by the military as an active-duty soldier or a civilian employee, you are eligible. If you take up employment with the military after the start of your scholarship, you would lose your eligibility.

If you served in the military but have been discharged (even if you are in obligatory reserve status) or if you worked for the military as a civilian but are no longer under contract with them, you are eligible.

It's also a bad idea to mention the intent to work with any organization that is affiliated with military research in the future. While not disqualifying, it can put your application under additional scrutiny, which is never a good thing.

Arrival in Japan

The Requirement

The requirement for the Embassy-Recommended MEXT Scholarship and University-Recommended MEXT Scholarship is identical:

> Those who cannot arrive in Japan during the period designated by MEXT or the accepting university.

Interpreting the Requirement

We covered the more detailed requirement about when you have to arrive earlier. But the requirement shows up again here: If you do not arrive during the specified time, MEXT would consider you to have voluntarily withdrawn from the scholarship.

Past Scholarship Receipt

The Requirement

The requirement for the Embassy-Recommended MEXT Scholarship and University-Recommended MEXT Scholarship are similar but with a few minor differences:

Embassy-Recommended MEXT Scholarship:

Those who are previous grantees of Japanese Government (MEXT) Scholarship programs (including those who withdraw from the scholarship program after the arrival in Japan). This does not apply to: those who have educational or work experience exceeding more than three years from the following month of the period of the previous scholarship to the estimated first month of the payment of this scholarship; and the past grantees of Japanese Studies Students program who have graduated or are going to graduate from universities in their home countries, Japan-Korea Joint Government Scholarship Program for the Students in Science and Engineering Departments and Young Leaders' Program. The Monbukagakusho Honors Scholarship for Privately-Financed International Students is not included in the Japanese Government (MEXT) Scholarship Programs;

University-Recommended MEXT Scholarship:

Those who are previous grantees of Japanese Government (MEXT) Scholarship programs (including those who withdraw from the scholarship program after acquisition of student status). However, this does not apply to those who wish to apply for Research Students program and meet any one of the following conditions. In addition, since the Monbukagakusho Honors Scholarship for Privately-Financed International Students does not apply to the Japanese Government (MEXT) Scholarship programs, the previous grantees can apply.

- those who have at least three years of educational or work experience following the end of the payment of the previous scholarship and the start of this scholarship;

- the past grantees of Japanese Studies Students program who have graduated or are going to graduate from universities in their home countries, Japan-Korea Joint Government Scholarship

Program for the Students in Science and Engineering Departments and Young Leaders' Program;

- those who have obtained or are expected to obtain a degree as undergraduate students of the Japanese Government (MEXT) Scholarship programs (university recommendation/special selection).

The difference is that the University-Recommended MEXT Scholarship makes an exception for past recipients of the University-Recommended MEXT Scholarship for undergraduate students under the PGP category. That exception exists because it is impossible to extend an undergraduate PGP scholarship, unlike all other undergraduate scholarship types, so a "new" scholarship is the only way for those students to continue their studies.

Interpreting the Requirement

Past receipt of Japanese government scholarships *does not* include the JASSO scholarship or the Monbukagakusho Honors Scholarship, so if you received any of those scholarships in the past, you are still eligible.

You only need to pay attention to this requirement if you received a MEXT scholarship in the past for degree-seeking studies in Japan.

You would also be ineligible even if you were awarded the scholarship but later withdrew *after* officially becoming a student in Japan. If you withdrew before arriving in Japan, then you would still be eligible. Remember that violating any of the eligibility criteria counts as "voluntary withdrawal" from the program.

The MEXT Japanese Studies Scholarship or the Japan-Korea Joint Government Scholarship Program for the Students in Science and Engineering Departments are both scholarships that apply to students enrolled in overseas universities who study abroad in Japan for part of their degrees. As long as you have returned to your home country and university and graduated from that university (or, if you are still enrolled, will graduate from that university before coming to Japan), that will not affect your eligibility.

If you have received a MEXT scholarship for a degree in Japan, other than the Young Leaders Program, then you will need to prove that you have sufficient experience from the end of that degree to the start of your new studies in Japan.

"Educational experience" in this context means enrollment at a university. Work experience refers to documentable full-time employment. Freelancing, solopreneurship, or part-time employment would not count.

Calculating Time between Programs

When calculating the time, you count from the first day you enrolled in education/started working or the first day of the month after your last scholarship payment, whichever comes later.

For example, let's say you completed a master's degree as a MEXT scholar and your last scholarship payment was in March 2022.

If you started full-time employment in April 2022 and continued to work for three full years, then you would be eligible to apply for a new scholarship starting in April 2025, assuming that you worked through to March 31, 2025.

If you started your job in May 2022, then by March 2025, you wouldn't wouldn't meet the requirement of three full years (two years, eleven months), so you could not apply for a new MEXT Scholarship for April 2025. You would be eligible after completing one more month of work, so you could apply for a scholarship starting in October 2025.

You can start your application before meeting the three-full-years requirement, but you would have to meet that requirement before arriving in Japan.

Concurrent MEXT Scholarship Application

The Requirement

The requirements for the Embassy-Recommended MEXT Scholarship and University-Recommended MEXT Scholarship have different wording, but are identical in intent.

Embassy-Recommended MEXT Scholarship:

> Those who are currently also applying to another program under the Japanese Government (MEXT) Scholarship system. This includes the programs for which scholarship payments will begin in FY2023, although their final selection results have not been decided yet, and the programs for which scholarship payments will begin in FY2024;

University-Recommended MEXT Scholarship:

> Those who are currently also applying to another program under the Japanese Government (MEXT) Scholarship system. This includes the programs for which scholarship payments will begin in FY2024;

The fiscal year references are from the 2023/2024 application guidelines. The specific year changes with each application cycle.

The difference in wording is because of the application timelines. The Embassy-Recommended MEXT Scholarship application period starts before the previous year's University-Recommended MEXT Scholarship application process releases its final results and continues through past the start of the next University-Recommended MEXT Scholarship.

By the time the University-Recommended MEXT Scholarship application begins, there is no possibility of unresolved application from the previous year.

Interpreting the Requirement

This eligibility requirement means you may not have multiple ongoing MEXT Scholarship applications, even if they are for different years. You cannot apply to multiple universities under the University-Recommended MEXT Scholarship, even if one application is for a PGP program and one is for general category, and you cannot apply for both the Embassy-Recommended and University-Recommended MEXT Scholarships at the same time.

You may apply for the University-Recommended MEXT Scholarship if you applied for the Embassy-Recommended MEXT Scholarship and did not pass the primary screening. If you have already been eliminated from the Embassy-Recommended MEXT Scholarship, then you would not be "currently also applying", since that application would have ended.

If you applied for the Embassy-Recommended MEXT Scholarship and passed the primary screening, then you would not be eligible to apply for the University-Recommended MEXT Scholarship. But since you are essentially guaranteed to receive the scholarship if you pass the embassy's primary screening, there would be no point in applying to the university, as well.

Likewise, if you applied for the University-Recommended MEXT Scholarship and the university nominated you to MEXT, you would not have your final, official result by the time the next year's Embassy-Recommended MEXT Scholarship started, so you would be ineligible, but you would be essentially guaranteed to receive the scholarship through the university, anyway.

Concurrent Enrollment in Japan (Embassy-Recommended MEXT Scholarship)

The Requirement

This requirement exists only for the Embassy-Recommended MEXT Scholarship:

Those who are already enrolled in a Japanese university or other institution with a residence status of "Student," or who are to be enrolled, or plan to be enrolled, in a Japanese university or other institution as a privately-financed international student from the time of application to the MEXT scholarship program in the applicant's country until the commencement of the period for payment of the MEXT scholarship. However, this stipulation does not apply to privately-financed international students who, are enrolled, or are planning to be enrolled, in a Japanese university or other institution but verifiably complete their studies before the start of the scholarship payment period and newly acquire the "Student" residence status;

Interpreting the Requirement

This requirement applies to applicants who are studying in Japan on a "Student" visa, without a specific end date to their studies. Its intent is to prevent applicants from enrolling in a Japanese university intending to drop out if they get the MEXT Scholarship and to prevent applicants from enrolling continuously in Japanese language schools in Japan while trying to get the MEXT Scholarship.

If you are not enrolled in a Japanese university or institution (e.g. language school) in Japan with a "Student" residence status, and do not intend to enroll in a Japanese university or institution with a "Student" residence status before the start of your MEXT-sponsored studies, this eligibility requirement does not apply to you.

If you are a self-financed student (including students financed by any other scholarship scheme besides a Japanese government scholarship) at a Japanese university at the time of application and will graduate and return to your home country before the start of your MEXT scholarship, you are also eligible.

If you are outside Japan, but want to come to Japan in the meantime to enroll in a Japanese university for any reason, such as language studies, you would either have to come on a "Temporary visitor" status (valid for 90 days or fewer) you would have to show that the program you plan to enroll in will be complete before your scholarship starts and that you will return to your home country between the end of that program and the start of the MEXT scholarship.

Basically, this eligibility requirement means you cannot use this application process to start funding a degree in Japan partway through and, if you are enrolled in a Japanese university already, you cannot stay enrolled and only quit if you get the scholarship. MEXT wants you to commit to the scholarship application. If you are enrolled in a university in another country, though, you can stay enrolled while waiting for the MEXT scholarship results.

I have seen cases where students applied and were accepted to Japanese universities as self-financed students, but then declined to enroll and applied for the MEXT scholarship, instead. That will not affect your eligibility.

Residence in Japan (University-Recommended MEXT Scholarship - General Category)

The Requirement

This requirement exists only for the General Category of the University-Recommended MEXT Scholarship:

> Those who are residing in Japan at the time of application.

My translation.

Interpreting the Requirement

Residing in Japan means you have a "residence status". Visiting Japan as a "Temporary visitor" (a stay of up to 90 days), would not make you ineligible, but if you reside in Japan on a "Student" residence status, "Dependent" residence status, a working status, etc., you are not eligible to apply for the University-Recommended MEXT Scholarship general category.

It is still possible to apply for the PGP category, at least as of the 2024/2025 cycle, but that category has a specific limit (40% of the total slots per PGP program, as of 2023/2024) to the number of domestic applicants allowed.

Concurrent Scholarship Receipt

The Requirement

The requirements for the Embassy-Recommended MEXT Scholarship and University-Recommended MEXT Scholarship were identical through 2023. In 2024, the Embassy-Recommended MEXT Scholarship guidelines changed and I expect the University-Recommended MEXT Scholarship guidelines will also change in 2024, although they are not yet available as of this publication, so I am listing the 2023 guidelines. Be sure to check the guidelines for your application year!

Embassy-Recommended MEXT Scholarship (2024):

Those who are planning to receive other scholarships or fellowships from Japanese government, a Japanese government-related organization and others after the start of the scholarship payment period;

University-Recommended MEXT Scholarship (2023):

Those who are planning to receive scholarship money from an organization other than MEXT (including a government organization of the applicant's country) on top of the scholarship money provided by MEXT after the start of the scholarship payment (the acquisition of student status);

As you can see, the 2024 change was to specify that only scholarships issued by another Japanese government or government-related organization are prohibited. The "and others" phrase in the explanation is a mistranslation of the Japanese. In Japanese, the restriction is limited to the Japanese government and government-related organizations.

The other difference is that University-Recommended MEXT Scholarship specifies that the acquisition of student status marks the start of the scholarship payment period. For the Embassy-Recommended MEXT Scholarship, you might spend your first semester in the Japanese language program at another university, so your acquisition of student status at the accepting university would come later.

Interpreting the Requirement

The 2023 requirement meant you could not accept other scholarships that cover the same line items as the MEXT Scholarship: Travel expenses to Japan, tuition, application fees, and/or living expenses. If you won the MEXT scholarship, you were required to cancel your application for any other scholarships you were seeking and withdraw from any other scholarship programs that had already selected you. For MEXT scholars with families, this included any scholarship programs awarded *to the scholar* to help cover their family's expenses while living in Japan. It would not include scholarships awarded to family members.

However, the 2024 change to the Embassy-Recommended MEXT Scholarship clarifies that you may receive other concurrent scholarships, as long as they do not come from the Japanese government. So a scholarship from your home country government or a private company in Japan, etc., would be allowed. I expect that this change will apply to the University-Recommended MEXT Scholarship when the 2024 version of those guidelines is released.

This requirement *does not* prevent you from applying for grants for specific research activities or conference attendance. MEXT scholars are still eligible to apply for grants to fund costs for their research projects or to defray the cost of travel to or participation in conferences during their studies in Japan, since those are things that the MEXT scholarship does not cover.

Failure to Graduate from Previous Degree

The Requirement

The requirement for the Embassy-Recommended MEXT Scholarship and University-Recommended MEXT Scholarship is identical:

> Those who are expected to graduate at the time of application and cannot satisfy the condition of academic background by the deadline given;

Interpreting the Requirement

If you have already graduated from your last degree program, this requirement does not apply to you.

This requirement only applies to applicants who have not yet graduated from their qualifying degree when applying for the MEXT scholarship. If you cannot complete your degree before coming to Japan for any reason, you would lose your eligibility and forfeit your scholarship.

Anyone who submits a "Certificate of Expected Graduation" during the application process will be required to show a "Certificate of Graduation" before starting their MEXT-funded studies.

A Certificate of Graduation does not need to be a diploma. A letter from your university stating that you have completed all of your requirements and will receive your degree at the next graduation ceremony is sufficient. So, if you complete all of your graduation requirements, but the diploma is late, that will not affect your eligibility if you can provide alternative documentation.

Japanese Dual Nationality

The Requirement

The requirement for the Embassy-Recommended MEXT Scholarship and University-Recommended MEXT Scholarship is identical:

> Holders of dual nationality at the time of application who cannot verify that they will give up

Japanese nationality by the time of the arrival in Japan (the acquisition of student status);

Interpreting the Requirement

This requirement only applies if one of your nationalities is Japanese. If you have, for example, French and Italian citizenship, this does not apply!

If you are a Japanese citizen with dual citizenship, you must be able to prove that you will surrender your Japanese citizenship before arriving in Japan.

Note that you do not have to surrender it before applying or before receiving the results. So, if you can, set the date to surrender your citizenship after MEXT releases the application results, so that you have time to change your mind if you do not win the scholarship!

Remember that these disqualification criteria will also result in your scholarship being canceled if MEXT discovers you to be in violation during your studies in Japan. So, if you don't surrender your Japanese nationality and it is discovered later, you would lose the scholarship.

Residence Status Other Than Student

The Requirement

As of the 2023/2024 application cycle, this was only a disqualification criteria for the Embassy-Recommended MEXT Scholarship application process. If is not a "disqualification criteria" in the University-Recommended MEXT Scholarship application process, but it is an item in the Monbukagakusho pledge form that you will sign after arrival in Japan, so the same requirement will apply:

> Those who change their residence status to that of other than "Student" after their arrival in Japan;

Interpreting the Requirement

As a MEXT scholar, you will apply for and receive a "Student" visa before coming to Japan and will be on a "Student" residence status throughout the time of your studies. Each month, you will need to report to your university in person and show your residence card, proving that you still have "Student" residence status before you can receive your monthly stipend.

There is no reason you would change during your studies. Even if you marry a Japanese citizen, you would have to stay a "Student" until the end of your degree and change to a "Spouse" status after the last scholarship payment.

The only time this requirement becomes an issue is when students are in their last month or two of their scholarship and have found a job in Japan that they want to start immediately after graduation. In order to work in Japan after graduation, you would need to change to a working residence status. However, as a MEXT scholar, you must not do so until after you have signed for your last scholarship payment, even if your employer wants you to change earlier than that.

Research or Internship Outside Japan

The Requirement

The requirement for the Embassy-Recommended MEXT Scholarship and University-Recommended MEXT Scholarship is identical:

> Those who plan to, from the time of application for the MEXT scholarship program, engage in long-term research (such as fieldwork or intern-

ship) outside Japan or plan to take a long-term leave of absence from the university;

Interpreting the Requirement

During your MEXT scholarship, you must focus on your studies in Japan and not take part in any activities that will take you away from the university.

One of your scholarship obligation is that you must be present at your university each month. As mentioned above, each month, you must show your Residence Card in person to prove that you are still studying at the university and still have a "Student" residence status and sign to receive your scholarship. If you do not sign during a particular month, you will not receive the scholarship stipend for that month. If you do not sign for three months in a row, you lose the scholarship.

When you apply for the scholarship, make sure that your research is to be conducted in Japan and that it does not require any fieldwork or internship to be conducted outside of Japan, and you will be fine! It is fine to leave during your studies for periods shorter than one month, such as to conduct brief fieldwork during a long vacation, but you should avoid having that as part of your initial proposal, if possible.

Non-degree Status Only (University-Recommended MEXT Scholarship - General Category)

The Requirement

This requirement exists only for the General category of the University-Recommended MEXT Scholarship:

> Those who have no intention to matriculate to the degree program.

My translation.

Interpreting the Requirement

You must intend to earn a degree from the university in Japan under the University-Recommended MEXT Scholarship. It is not possible to use the MEXT Scholarship to come to Japan just to work on research for a degree that you will earn from a foreign university.

No Intent to Obtain Degree

The Requirement

The requirements for the Embassy-Recommended MEXT Scholarship and University-Recommended MEXT Scholarship are essentially identical:

> Those who have no intention to obtain a degree in Japan;

The words "in Japan" are not present in the University-Recommended MEXT Scholarship guidelines, but the same meaning is implied, since you would be enrolled in a degree program.

Interpreting the Requirement

Even if you will start your studies in Japan as a non-regular student, you must intend to matriculate to the degree program and graduate. If that goal ever changes, then you would lose the scholarship.

Cheating (Embassy-Recommended MEXT Scholarship)

The Requirement

This requirement exists only for the Embassy-Recommended MEXT Scholarship:

> Those who are found to have attempted or actually committed any kinds of cheating prohibited by the examiner during the written examination of the First Screening.

Interpreting the Requirement

During the Embassy-Recommended MEXT Scholarship primary screening or First Screening, you will take Japanese and English language proficiency tests at the embassy. Cheating or attempted cheating on those tests will get you disqualified.

End of the Disqualification Criteria

This concludes the list of disqualification criteria.

Remember, disqualification criteria are written in such a way that if you *meet* any of the criteria, you are not eligible.

For all the remaining criteria, you *must meet* the criteria to be eligible.

Field of Study

The Requirement

There are significant differences between the wording of the requirements for the Embassy-Recommended MEXT Scholarship and the University-Recommended MEXT Scholarship, but as we'll cover below, *most* of the same requirements apply.

Embassy-Recommended MEXT Scholarship:

Applicants should apply for the field of study they majored in at university or its related field. Moreover, the fields of study must be subjects which applicants will be able to study and research in graduate courses at Japanese universities. The fields of study may be restricted to particular fields by the Japanese Embassy or Consulate (hereinafter referred to "Japanese diplomatic mission") in the applicant's country. Traditional entertainment arts such as Kabuki and classical Japanese dances, or subjects that require practical training in specific technologies or techniques at factories or companies are not included in the fields of study under this scholarship program.

A student who studies medicine, dentistry or welfare science will not be allowed to engage in clinical training such as medical care and operative surgery until he/she obtains a relevant license from the Minister of Health, Labor and Welfare under applicable Japanese laws.

University-Recommended MEXT Scholarship:

Applicants should apply for the field of study they majored in at university or its related field. Moreover, the fields of study must be subjects which applicants will be able to study and research at the accepting universities.

As you can see, the Embassy-Recommended MEXT Scholarship requirements are much more specific, but this is because applicants' universities are not yet determined. MEXT expects that almost everything included in the embassy requirements would also be evaluated by the university prior to your selection.

Interpreting the Requirement

There are so many elements rolled up in here that it is easy to get lost. Let's take it step by step.

1. You must apply in a field that you have majored in at university or in a related field.

Based on the number of questions I have seen on my website, this might just be the most difficult eligibility requirement to understand. So if you're confused, you're not alone.

If you are applying in a field that was your major upon graduation from a previous university, at the undergraduate or graduate level, you will be fine. If you had multiple majors or have earned degrees in different majors, you can apply in any of those fields. If you majored in a field in a degree that you *did not* complete, there is no clear rule, so it would be subject to the embassy or university's discretion. That means you need to have your justification in order!

The tricky part is understanding what counts as a "related field". Depending on whether you are in social sciences/arts/humanities or STEM, you could see more or less flexibility. Interdisciplinary majors (like Area Studies) would have the easiest time because they could choose any of the fields they covered under the umbrella of the interdisciplinary major.

In either humanities, social sciences, or STEM, sub-fields, or fields that cover similar contents are "related fields". For example, if you majored in political science for your bachelor's degree and wanted to study international relations in graduate school under the MEXT scholarship, that would be acceptable. International relations is a subset of political science and there is significant overlap. The same would go from changing from mechanical engineering to robotics.

But what about more drastic changes? It all comes down to your ability to justify it.

Some of the most common significant field changes I see are changing from an "unrelated" undergraduate degree to an MBA or a degree in computer science, or vice versa. In those cases, applicants often justify the change by focusing on how they will use the MBA to explore business applications of their previous studies, or use the computer science degree to apply data science to a problem they previously studied. Of course, in either of those cases, it would help if you had some experience taking relevant courses, as well.

Even if your fields are even more distant, it is still possible if you make the case.

An applicant whose undergraduate degree was in neurobiology once asked me if it would be possible to switch to graphic design. Those seem pretty distant, and I have no expertise in either, but with a heavy dose of creativity, it might just be possible.

If that applicant had done research into recovery from brain trauma and had discovered that certain visual patterns could stimulate the development of new synapse pathways in the brain, then perhaps the applicant could have spun that into a justification into studying graphic design with that specific context in mind.

If you are trying to make a far-fetched connection, then brainstorm ideas early and go over them with colleagues from each field. If you are still enrolled in your previous degree, start brainstorming transition pathways early, so that you can steer your research for the rest of your studies and further justify the transition.

2. The field of study must be available at Japanese universities (in the language you meet the proficiency requirements for).

Before you decide on your field of study and start writing your field of study and research program plan, identify the university (or up to three universities for the Embassy-Recommended MEXT Scholarship) that you want to apply to and the professor(s) you want to study under.

You need to make sure there is a graduate program at a Japanese university that teaches your field of study and that the language of instruction is one you are qualified to study in. In Book 3 of this series, I describe how to find the best university and advisor for your studies, including how to search for university programs taught in English. I also have an article about how to find English-taught degree programs in Japan at the link below that can be a good start for finding relevant programs in your field.

- Book: *How to Find Your Best Degree Program and Advisor for the MEXT Scholarship*
  https://mymext.com/getmms3

- Article: "How to Find Universities and Professors in Japan (MEXT Scholarship)"
  https://mymext.com/professors

If you can only find programs taught in Japanese, you will need to be fluent in Japanese, even if there are faculty members there who speak English. All of your classes and assignments, including your thesis or dissertation, would be in Japanese. If you find yourself in that situation, research what level of Japanese language ability is required for self-financed international student applicants to that program and ensure that you meet or exceed that requirement.

As long as you have researched target universities and found at least one degree program taught in English that you want to apply to, you will meet this part of the requirement.

Of course, you would need to have that information in hand before completing an application for the University-Recommended MEXT Scholarship, but it applies to the Embassy-Recommended MEXT Scholarship, too. Make sure that you know what programs are taught in English before completing your Placement Preference Form!

3. For the Embassy-Recommended MEXT Scholarship, they may limit which fields are available to applicants from specific countries, based on the needs of that country and agreements in place between the Japanese government and the local government.

4. For medical or dental programs that require a practicum, you would need to be fluent in Japanese in order to obtain the licenses required to practice or take part in a residency.

5. Programs that are specifically not covered, like Kabuki from the Embassy-Recommended MEXT Scholarship requirement, are subjects that are not taught in graduate programs at Japanese universities, anyway. Those fields are more appropriate to colleges of technology or specialized training, which are not covered by the MEXT scholarship for research students.

The reference to Japanese traditional performing arts being excluded means you cannot train to become a performer under this scholarship. This distinction is more clear in the original Japanese version of the requirement. You would still be eligible to enroll in an *academic program* to research performing arts, just as you would in a program that researches literature, etc.

Prohibited Fields of Study: Weapons and Dual-use Technology

Besides the clear requirements for the field of study, there is a "secret" requirement as well: All research related to the development or production of weapons of mass destruction or research into technology that could be used for the development or production of weapons of mass destruction is prohibited. Fortunately, this should be easy to avoid.

Like other "secret" eligibility requirements, you will not find this in the eligibility to *apply* for the MEXT scholarship. It is in the eligibility requirements for embassies or universities to *recommend* applicants for the scholarship.

You will be allowed to apply, but if your research field falls under the prohibition below, you would not be accepted.

The Requirement

(From the requirements for universities to submit nominees to MEXT)

Universities must be familiar with the Japanese government's policy toward research related to the illegal exportation of goods or research that could be related to weapons of mass destruction and in the case of applicants who express a desire to conduct research in a field that could contribute to the production or development of weapons of mass destruction, must carefully evaluate the applicant's research plan and academic background through interviews, etc., and must not nominate such applicants. Universities must also give full attention to the "Foreign Country User List" and "Guidance for the Control of Sensitive Technologies for Security Export for Academic and Research Institutions" published by the Ministry of Economics, Trade and Industry.

*My translation. (References to the government policy documents mentioned in the eligibility requirement omitted.)

The references in the original requirement include a 108-page document in Japanese on the export of technology related to weapons of mass destruction. For the sake of brevity, I will not translate that here.

Interpreting the Requirement

As long as you are not seeking to conduct research that could be used for creating biological or chemical weapons, nuclear weapons, or rocketry, you should be fine. But even if your research is not specifically related to weapons technology, avoid any references to organization that are known for affiliation with weapons research.

As mentioned in the section on Japanese performing arts above, this requirement does not prevent you from researching related academic topics. For example, you could still research nuclear weapons proliferation from an international relations perspective. The only prohibition is on researching the technology.

Current Residence in Japan

The Requirement

As of the 2023/2024 application, the requirement (in English) is different for the Embassy-Recommended MEXT Scholarship and for the two types (General category and PGP) of the University-Recommended MEXT Scholarship.

Embassy-Recommended MEXT Scholarship:

An applicant shall, in principle, newly obtain a "Student" visa at the overseas establishment of Japan located in the applicant's country of nationality, and enter Japan with the residence status of "Student." If the applicant lives in Japan exceptionally under a residence status other than "Student" before acceptance, the applicant must change his/her status to "Student" by the end of the previous month before the installment of scholarship payment. **The applicant should be aware that after expiration of the status as a MEXT Scholarship student and even if the student again applies for their original resident status of "Permanent resident" or "Long-term resident," the such resident statuses might**

not be necessarily granted. Moreover, as the Japanese government requires pre-arrival tuberculosis screening for some countries, applicants obtaining a visa shall follow guidance at the overseas establishment of Japan located in the applicant's country of nationality.

The section in bold appears only in Japanese in 2023/2024 and is bold in that document, too. It appeared in previous English versions, as well and I have used the text from one of those years.

University-Recommended MEXT Scholarship (General Category):

An applicant shall, in principle, newly obtain a "Student" visa at the overseas establishment of Japan located in the applicant's country of nationality, and enter Japan with the residence status of "Student." If the applicant lives in Japan exceptionally under a residence status other than "Student" before acceptance, the applicant must change his/her status to "Student" by the end of the previous month before the installment of scholarship payment. The applicant should be aware that after expiration of the status as a MEXT Scholarship student and even if the student again applies for their original resident status of "Permanent resident" or "Long-term resident," the such resident statuses might not be necessarily granted.

Moreover, as the Japanese government requires pre-arrival tuberculosis screening for some countries, applicants obtaining a visa shall follow guidance at the overseas establishment of Japan located in the applicant's country of nationality.

The application guidelines are only in Japanese, but the Japanese is identical to the phrasing of the requirements for the Embassy-Recommended MEXT Scholarship, so I have used that translation.

University-Recommended MEXT Scholarship (PGP):

An applicant shall, in principle, newly obtain a "Student" visa at the Japanese diplomatic mission located in the applicant's country of nationality, and enter Japan with the residence status of "Student."

Please also note that if a grantee arrives in Japan without newly obtaining a "Student" visa, scholarship payments will be canceled. Moreover, as the Japanese government requires pre-arrival tuberculosis screening for some countries, applicants obtaining a visa shall follow guidance at the overseas establishment of Japan located in the applicant's country of nationality.

* Visa requirements and status of residence for domestic recommenders

For those whose current status of residence is not "Student," applicants must change their status of residence to "Student" at the local Immigration Services Agency in Japan by time of registration as students at the accepting university. Even in cases of having other statuses of residence ("Permanent Resident," "Long-term Resident", etc.), applicants must change their status to "Student" and begin their courses of study as Japanese Government (MEXT) Scholarship students. It is important to note that applications for "Permanent Resident" or "Long-term Resident" status after status of Japanese Government (MEXT) Scholarship student ends, may not be granted as a matter of course. Also, if studies as Japanese Government (MEXT) Scholarship students begin without changing status of residence to "Student," scholarships will be canceled.

For those whose current status of residence is

"Student," they must complete the renewal procedures before the expiration of their periods of stay. Additionally, in the event of changes in school enrollment, notification must be submitted pursuant to the provisions of Article 19-16 of the Immigration-Control and Refugee-Recognition Act.

Interpreting the Requirement (Not living in Japan)

"Residing" means living in Japan with a mid- to long-term residence status, where you would register at the local city hall and would have a Residence Card issued by the Japanese government.

If you are not residing in Japan, and have no plans to reside in Japan before enrolling in your MEXT-funded degree, you do not need to worry about this requirement. Traveling to Japan as a tourist (Temporary visitor visa or visa-free stay) at any point during your application, the screening, or prior to starting your scholarship is also not a problem. So, it would be possible, for example, to come to Japan briefly to meet with prospective advisors at Japanese universities or to take an in-person entrance exam related to the scholarship application.

The only concern for most applicants is that you must also be eligible to apply for and receive a student visa for Japan. This means that there must be no restrictions on your ability to leave your home country and no restrictions on your ability to get a visa to enter Japan. The only reasons that would prevent you from obtaining a visa to enter Japan are a history of deportation from Japan (or departure on a Departure Order) or being an internationally wanted criminal or terrorist.

I have also heard of cases where applicants have been prevented from applying for a visa by their home country governments, such as in cases of public servants who have a service time requirement, but that is quite rare.

Interpreting the Requirement (Living in Japan)

Where this requirement gets complicated is for applicants who are living in Japan at the time of application. This requirement seems to be indirect conflict with other parts of the application guidelines in some places.

There are two categories for how you may be living in Japan at the time of application, at least as far as the scholarship is concerned:

1. **"Student" resident status:** If you came to Japan to study and are enrolled in a high school, university, language school, etc. Here, you would have a projected end time to your studies, after which you would have to leave Japan.

2. **Any other resident status:** The most common examples would be "Permanent Resident", "Long-term Resident", or "Dependent", though you might also have a working visa of some kind or be the "Spouse or Child of a Japanese National".

If you are in category 1 ("Student"), you can apply for the Embassy-Recommended MEXT Scholarship (note that you would have to travel in person to the Japanese embassy in your home country for parts of the application process) or the PGP Category of the University-Recommended MEXT Scholarship as one of the "Domestic recommenders" slots. In either case, you would return to your home country at the end of your current studies and apply for a new "Student" visa as a MEXT scholar. If your current studies continue until the start of your MEXT Scholarship, then you could apply for an "Extension of Period of Stay" to extend your "Student" residence status to cover your MEXT Scholarship period.

If you are applying for the General Category of the University-Recommended MEXT Scholarship, the eligibility requirements say that if you are residing in Japan at the time of application, you are not eligible to apply. However, it also says that students who "are expected to graduate" from undergraduate programs in Japan as recipients of the PGP University-Recommended MEXT Scholarship for undergraduate students *are* eligible to apply. These statements are contradictory, since being "expected to graduate" from a

Japanese university would mean that you are enrolled there and living in Japan, and there is no additional information about exceptions. If you are in this situation, please consult with the university where you are enrolled and ask them to contact MEXT, if necessary.

If you are in category 2 (anything other than student), you can apply for the Embassy-Recommended MEXT Scholarship (note that you would have to travel in person to the Japanese embassy in your home country for parts of the application process) or the PGP Category of the University-Recommended MEXT Scholarship as one of the "Domestic recommenders" slots, just like category 1. The important things to note are the deadline to change your residence status to "Student" and your status after graduation.

The part of the requirement about your previous residence status not being granted means it is not automatic that you would be able to return to a status like "Permanent Resident" or "Long-term Resident", even if you held one of those statuses before the MEXT Scholarship. Assume that you would have to apply for the status again and meet all the eligibility requirements just like a first time applicant. Some of the "Long-term Resident" statuses are only valid before you reach the age of majority/adulthood, so you could not return to those statuses after your MEXT studies. If you are in this situation, I recommend you consider what you will do to maintain your residence in Japan after graduation and make sure that it is worth it to you to apply for the scholarship.

Grade Point Average (GPA)

Typically, you will not find the GPA (grades, average marks, weighted average, etc.) requirement listed anywhere in the eligibility criteria, whether you are applying for the Embassy or University-Recommended MEXT Scholarship. However, the standard exists for all Japanese government scholarships, including the MEXT Scholarship and JASSO Scholarship. For the University-Recommended MEXT Scholarship, at least, MEXT's instruction to universities state they cannot recommend anyone that does not meet this requirement. (MEXT's instructions to embassies are not available to the public, so I cannot confirm their contents.)

To be eligible to be nominated for the MEXT scholarship, you must have a minimum of a converted 2.3 GPA on MEXT's unique 3.0 scale. We will go over how to convert your academic performance to this scale below and you can find sample conversion tables in Appendix A.

The first important thing for you to understand is how GPA factors in the application process. GPA is a minimum eligibility requirement to *be nominated* for the scholarship, not to *apply*.

What difference does this make? If you do not meet one of the eligibility requirements to *apply* that I described above, then the Embassy or University could not accept your application for review. In that situation, they would have to return your application materials to you and explain why do not meet the eligibility requirements to apply.

If you do not meet the *nomination* requirements, then the Embassy or University is under no obligation to refuse your application and return your documents. You will not pass. You will not get an explanation and you will not get your documents back. So, given the different obligations, it only makes sense to include application eligibility requirement that the reviewers can evaluate quickly and explain to rejected applicants.

Converting every applicant's GPA, grades, marks, weighted average, etc., from the home university's scale to the MEXT scale is a time-consuming process. Sometimes, your grades are going to be in sealed envelopes, which could only be opened after the university officially receives your application. So it is not possible to include it in the eligibility criteria.

If you meet the eligibility requirements to apply, but not the eligibility requirements to be nominated (GPA), then the university or embassy can accept your application for review. At the end of the application screening (the document screening, for the embassy), they will simply tell you that you did not pass. In that situation, they do not need to tell you why or return anything to you. You would never know if your GPA was holding you back.

Fortunately, we're going to go over how to calculate your GPA now, so you should know if you are eligible before you even start the application.

Embassy-Recommended MEXT Scholarship: Local Grade Requirements

As we will cover below, embassies in each country may set their own additional eligibility requirements, as well. Some will choose to set a minimum grade requirement in your home country's system.

In that case, abide by that requirement in addition to MEXT's 2.3 out of 3.0 requirement, even if they are not an exact match. Usually, they are designed to match, but it is not possible to convert overall grades, so it will always be an approximation. If you are close to the requirement threshold given in your home country's system, calculate your MEXT GPA on your own to make sure you meet both requirements. Even if you are not close, I recommend calculating your MEXT GPA even if you are not close to the local threshold. Doing so will let you know how competitive your application will be.

Calculating Your GPA

You're going to need to get your academic transcript and the My MEXT Scholarship GPA Spreadsheet I sent you when you downloaded the bonus documents. If you haven't gotten

those yet, you can grab them now from the link below:
https://mymext.com/bonusmms1

You can also do this with a pencil and calculator.

For the sake of simplicity, I am going to use "transcript" to refer to the document or documents that show your academic performance in each of your classes. Depending on your country's or university's system, this document might have a different name, such as "marks sheet". The important thing to remember is that it is the official document, issued by the university, that shows your academic performance for each class you took.

But first, let's get clear on what counts for the calculation.

When converting your grades to the 3.0 system, MEXT only includes the grades you earned during degree-seeking program. If you are enrolled in a degree program, only the grades from that degree will count. If you are not enrolled in a degree program, then the grades from your most recent university degree would count.

There is one exception to this calculation. If your relevant degree program does not issue any grades, such as a research-only master's degree program. In that case, your Letter of Recommendation from the Dean (or higher) of your last university would have to show that you were in the top 30% of your class at the university or faculty level.

If your GPA can be calculated and is less than 2.30, then a letter saying that you were in the top 30% would not make you eligible. It only works if you have no grades available whatsoever.

The following grades do not count:

- Grades such as "pass" in a pass/fail course do not count. Grades of "fail" in a pass/fail class should not count if it is clear from your transcript that the class was pass/fail. They will count if it is not obvious that the course was pass/fail. Some universities may include them, anyway, so if you have any grades that meet that criteria, include them in the calculation, just in case, to see the worst-case scenario.

- Grades earned in a class that awarded zero credits or zero graduation credits. *If your university shows failed courses as being worth zero credits on your transcript, those grades would still count. And the number of credits for GPA calculation would be equal to the number that you would have earned if you had passed.

- You studied abroad during the past two years and your study abroad grades transferred back to your home university as pass/fail grades. You will probably have to turn in the transcript from your study abroad, but if the grades are not reflected on the transcript of the university you graduated from, they will not count.

- If you transferred universities during your last degree, then only grades earned *after* your transfer will count, but you will still need to submit official transcripts from all universities that you attended.

How to Calculate Your GPA on the MEXT Scale

You'll need to determine what scale to use to convert your grades from your university's scale to MEXT's 3.0 system. The charts in Appendix A show several sample conversions, along with images of the original grading system taken from the transcripts. Find the one that best matches your grading system.

The My MEXT Scholarship GPA Spreadsheet: Entering the Conversion Table

If you are using the My MEXT Scholarship GPA Spreadsheet, enter your conversions in the conversion table section. You'll need to enter every grade available on your system on the left and the converted MEXT grade on the right. Here's an example based on a system with grades A-D and F, where plus and minus grades are both considered subsets of the letter grade.

Conversion Table	
A+	3
A	3
A-	3
B+	3
B	3
B-	3
C+	2
C	2
C-	2
D+	1
D	1
D-	1
F	0

If you have a grade that you are not sure how to convert (for example, I have seen universities use the grade "B/C") then I recommend converting it to the lower possible score. Your calculation will not be final and official. You are only doing this now to make sure that you meet the minimum requirement, so be harsh on yourself.

Entering the Grades

Next, enter the grade you earned and the course weight in each line of the Grade Table. Your converted GPA will calculate automatically. You do not need to enter the course titles, unless you want to do so for your own reference.

Course weight means how much the course counts toward your graduation.

In some university systems (including Japan), you have to acquire a certain number of credits in order to graduate. In that case, your course weight is the credit value of the course. If your university requires you to acquire a certain number of marks to graduate and uses weighted marks, then your course weight would be the maximum number of marks available in that course.

If your university only requires that you complete a certain number of courses and does not weight any course more than another, then your course weight for each course would be "1".

Here's an example of entering the grades into the Grade Table. You only have to enter the grades in your home system. The sheet will do all the calculations for you.

Grade Table		
Course Name	**Local Grade**	**Weight**
Course 1	A+	3
Course 2	B	3
Course 3	C	3
Course 4	B+	3
Course 5	A	3
Course 6	A-	6
Course 7	B+	3
Course 8	B	3

Calculating Your GPA by Hand

If you are not using the My MEXT Scholarship GPA Spreadsheet, you can do the same calculation by hand with a calculator and pencil. I recommend making a photocopy of your transcript and writing on that.

Once you have your conversion scale, convert each grade, one-by-one to the equivalent grade on MEXT's scale. Then multiply the MEXT scale by the course weight to get the point value for the course. You cannot convert your overall average, as that will give you an inaccurate result. (See the sample calculations in Appendix B for an illustration of why this is the case.)

Add up all the point values and all the course weights, then divide the total point value by the total weight value to get your result. Here's how it would look with the 8 courses I listed above:

Grade Table				
Course Name	Local Grade	Weight	MEXT Grade	Point Value
Course 1	A+	3	3	9
Course 2	B	3	3	9
Course 3	C	3	2	6
Course 4	B+	3	3	9
Course 5	A	3	3	9
Course 6	A-	6	3	18
Course 7	B+	3	3	9
Course 8	B	3	3	9
Total		27		78
GPA	(Total Point Value / Total Weight)		(78/27)	2.88

For the result, you drop any numbers beyond the second decimal point. Do not round!

If you do the calculation above yourself, you'll see that the answer is 2.88888888... This does not become 2.89, it stays 2.88. At that score, it doesn't make a difference, but if your GPA calculated out to 2.2988888888 instead, then you could not round it to 2.30 (eligible), it would stay 2.29 (ineligible).

Embassy-Imposed Additional Requirements

If you are applying for the Embassy-Recommended MEXT Scholarship, there may be additional eligibility requirements.

Each Japanese embassy, in consultation with your country's local government, may impose additional eligibility restrictions. For example, they may require that you meet a minimum GPA in your home country's scale or they may limit the scholarship to specific fields of study.

Since this is decided on a country-by-country basis, the only way to find out if there are additional requirements for your country is to check with the local Japanese embassy or consulate.

Universities may also impose additional eligibility criteria, both for the Embassy-Recommended MEXT Scholarship and the University-Recommended MEXT Scholarship. In my experience, however, the only restrictions they tend to add are language proficiency requirements, particularly for programs taught in Japanese, or additional test requirements, such as GRE or GMAT scores. To find out if this is the case at the university or universities that you want to apply to, you'll have to check their websites.

Eligibility - Conclusion

That wraps up the list of eligibility criteria as of the 2024/2025 Embassy-Recommended MEXT Scholarship and the 2023/2024 University-Recommended MEXT Scholarship. If you are applying in a future year, be sure to check the requirements in the application guidelines for your year yourself, since they may change. (There have already been significant changes between when I published the first edition of this book in 2018 and the second in 2024.)

Here's the moment of truth: How did you do?

If you've just been reading through so far, and haven't stopped to review the criteria, use the worksheet on the next page, or the one in the downloadable bonus documents and do a self-review, now. There's no sense in moving on until you've made sure you can.

If you meet all the criteria we've reviewed, congratulations! There is nothing standing between you and winning the scholarship, as long as you are willing to put in the work. We'll start with that in the next chapter, as we discuss your application strategy.

If you did not meet all the eligibility criteria, I am sorry to hear that. Unfortunately, that happens. At least you know now, before spending countless hours on your application, not to mention money for tests and postage. You can focus on other opportunities instead. I wish you the best of luck!

Exercise 3: Eligibility

Answering the questions below will help you ensure you are eligible for the scholarship and clear up any doubts or questions you might have about eligibility.

As before, you can fill out your answers in a notebook or download the exercise worksheets that go with the book at:

https://mymext.com/bonusmms1

1. What is the last degree you earned? Or, if you are still enrolled in a degree program, what level is that degree and when will you finish all of your graduation requirements?
Level: / Completion Date:

2. Have you earned, or will you earn, the prerequisite degree before arriving in Japan (Earned a bachelor's degree for master's applicants or a master's degree for doctoral applicants)? Yes / No

Your answer to question 2 must be "Yes" to be eligible.

3. Do you have Japanese nationality? No / Yes
3.a. If yes, are you a dual national and willing to surrender your Japanese nationality? Yes / No

If you answered "Yes" to question 3 and "No" to question 3.a, you are not eligible to apply. Any other combination of answers is eligible.

4. Does your country of nationality have diplomatic relations with Japan? Yes / No

Your answer to question 4 must be "Yes" to be eligible.

5. What year are you applying?
5.a. What calendar year will you start your studies in Japan?
5.b. Subtract 35 from 5.a.
5.c. Is your date of birth on or after April 2 of the year you calculated in 5.b.? Yes / No

Your answer to question 5.c must be "Yes" to be eligible.

6. Do you have any health conditions that require you to stay in your home country for treatment and would prevent you from studying in Japan? No / Yes

Your answer to question 6 must be "No" to be eligible.

7. Do you have language proficiency test scores for the language you plan to study in? Yes / No
7.a. Did you complete (or will you complete) your prerequisite degree in the language of the program in Japan (Japanese or English)? Yes / No
7.b. If you answered "No" to 7 and 7.a. above and you are not a native speaker, when is the next TOEFL iBT/IELTS/JLPT test in your area?

Reference:

- TOEFL iBT Online Portal:
  https://mymext.com/toefl

- IELTS Test Dates and Locations:
  https://mymext.com/ielts

- JLPT Test Dates and Locations:
  https://mymext.com/jlpt

Note: MEXT accepts completion of your prerequisite degree in the same language as proof of language ability, but some universities may not. Check the specific requirements for the universities where you want to study!

8. In what ways could you leverage your research to contribute to the local community (e.g. giving presentations or lessons to community groups, working on specific projects)?

9. Are you willing to get involved in visits to schools and public organizations or volunteer at festivals and events while in Japan? Yes / No

10. Is there any reason (work, school, inability to obtain passport) that you could not leave your home country during the time specified by MEXT to arrive in Japan? No / Yes

Your answer to question 10 must be "No" to be eligible.

11. Have you ever been deported from Japan or left Japan under a Departure Order in the past? No / Yes

11.a. If you answered "Yes" to question 11, you will have a specific period during which you may not reenter Japan. When does that period end?

11.b. Would your studies start after that date? Yes / No

Your answer to question 11 must be "No" or your answer to question 11.b must be "Yes" to be eligible.

12. Are you currently an active-duty member of the military or a civilian employed by the military? No / Yes

12.a. If you answered yes to question 9, are you able to be discharged or released from your contract before you would start your studies in Japan? Yes / No

Your answer to question 12 must be "No" or your answer to question 12.a must be "Yes" to be eligible.

13. Have you received a MEXT scholarship (other than the Japanese Studies Scholarship, the Japan-Korea Joint Government Scholarship Program For The Students In Science and Engineering Departments, or the Young Leaders Program) in the past? No / Yes

13.a. If you answered "Yes" to question 13, what was the last month when you received a scholarship payment?

13.b. How many complete months of university enrollment or full-time employment do you have since that date, starting with the month after your last payment?

Your answer to question 13 must be "No" or your answer to question 13.b must be "36" or higher to be eligible.

14. (University-Recommended MEXT Scholarship, only) Do you plan to apply to only one university this year via the University-Recommended MEXT Scholarship process, regardless of scholarship category? Yes / No

Your answer to question 14 must be "Yes" to be eligible.

15. Do you have any ongoing MEXT Scholarship application for which you have not received your final results (e.g. previous year's application or ongoing Embassy-Recommended MEXT Scholarship application)? Yes / No / I applied but was rejected (did not pass one of the screenings)

If your answer to question 15 is "Yes", you will not be eligible to apply again until the results of the current application are final.

16. Are you enrolled in a Japanese university or other institution and residing in Japan with a "Student" residence status? No / Yes

16.a. If you answered "Yes" to question 16, will you graduate and return to your home country before the start of the degree program that you are applying to via the MEXT scholarship? Yes / No

Your answer to question 16 must be "No" or your answer to question 16.a must be "Yes" to be eligible.

17. Do you plan to enroll in a Japanese university or other institution in Japan as a self-financed student and reside in the country with a "Student" residence status between the time you apply for the MEXT scholarship and when you arrive in Japan to start your scholarship-funded studies? No / Yes

Your answer to question 17 must be "No" to be eligible.

18. (University-Recommended MEXT Scholarship, General Category, only) Are you residing in Japan with a residence status other than "Temporary Visitor"? No / Yes

Your answer to question 18 must be "No" to be eligible.

19. Are you applying for or have you been selected for any other scholarships from the Japanese government that will provide money for tuition, living expenses, travel costs to Japan, etc., during your time as a MEXT scholar? No / Yes

If you answered "Yes" to question 19, you must be prepared to cancel your application or withdraw from the award for any other scholarships. (But not for grants for specific pro-jects, etc.)

20. Does your research plan require you to conduct field research or take part in an internship outside of Japan? No / Yes

Your answer to question 20 must be "No" to be eligible.

21. Do you plan to take a leave of absence at any time during your studies? No / Yes

Your answer to question 21 must be "No" to be eligible.

22. Is it your intention to earn a degree (at least) from a Japanese university as a MEXT scholar? Yes / No

Your answer to question 22 must be "Yes" to be eligible.

23. Describe how your intended field of study in Japan is related to your major or to research you have already conducted at university.

24. Write the name of at least one university in Japan that teaches your field of study at the degree level you want in a language you are qualified to speak. You can find information about how to search for programs taught in English at the link below:

https://mymext.com/professors

25. Does your research concern materials or technology that could be used for the development or production of weapons of mass destruction? No / Yes

Your answer to question 25 must be "No" to be eligible.

26. Calculate your GPA using the My MEXT Scholarship GPA Spreadsheet (or by hand). You can download the spreadsheet from:

https://mymext.com/bonusmms1

What is your GPA (maximum 2 decimal places)?

Your answer to question 26 must be 2.30 or higher to be eligible.

Chapter Four

Your Application Strategy

N ow that you understand the MEXT scholarship and benefits and have confirmed that you are eligible, it is time to plan your application strategy.

It is not enough to be an excellent student and have a great research idea. That might get you the scholarship and it might not. I don't know about you, but "might" is not good enough for me. Actually, I think I do know about you. You're reading a book about improving your chances of winning the scholarship. So, I'm assuming you also don't want to settle for "might" and want to take every step to increase your chances.

As discussed in the chapter on the successful applicant mentality, you need to approach the application process as a professional. A professional leaves nothing to chance. A professional learns everything he or she can about the challenge ahead and takes steps to prepare.

Applying for the MEXT scholarship is like a soccer match or a sumo tournament. If you want to win, you need to know the rules of the game, you need a good coach to get you ready, and you and your coach need a plan of attack that will help you maximize the benefits of your strengths and control the flow of the game to ensure your victory.

I'm here to be your coach, so let's get started with your game plan.

Your Theme: How You Will Serve

The first step in any game plan is deciding what outcome you want. In other words, your goal. If you don't have a goal, then you don't know what you're working toward and any effort you make might be in the wrong direction.

Let's get one thing out of the way:

Your goal is *not* to win the MEXT scholarship. Your goal is *what comes after you graduate.*

Japan does not award the MEXT scholarship just to fund students or degrees. The Japanese government wants to identify and support applicants who have the best chance of making a positive impact in the world - in line with the Japanese government's own objectives, of course - and becoming leaders in their countries and communities. Japan wants these leaders and innovators in countries around the world to be connected back to Japan, both through personal relationships and through a sense of appreciation.

If that tarnishes your image of what you thought was a purely academic effort, good. That's an important step in understanding your strategy. You need to know what the Japanese government wants.

Fortunately for you, what the Japanese government wants is outstanding global citizens who have a connection with

Japan. If you're applying for a graduate degree in Japan, then that's what you want to become, whether or not you realized it before.

So, what is your goal?

Let's start with your theme.

The core of your MEXT scholarship application strategy, which we will call your application theme, is deciding what difference you want to make in the world. Keep it to a single sentence, to start.

How do you want to serve the world?

Do you want to contribute to peace between nations? Alleviating poverty? Food security? Education? Environmental sustainability? Promoting understanding between cultures?

Your theme does not have to be obviously related to your field of research. I know a young woman who majored in photography, but her theme for serving the world was marine conservation. She once told me she regretted not majoring in something like marine biology. But as a photographer with a passion in that area, she could do things for marine conservation that a biologist might not be able to do, like raise awareness through emotional photojournalism and building a movement. Don't trap yourself with false limitations.

Once you have your theme, write it down. Use the exercise at the end of this chapter or the downloadable worksheets. There is something powerful about putting themes and goals down on paper, especially by hand. The process of writing it strengthens the goal in your head and having it articulated on paper will take you much closer to reaching your goal than keeping it in your head. We're going to be writing your theme at the top of almost every paper related to your strategy and, later, on all the worksheets related to your Field of Study and Research Program Plan.

If you have multiple ways you want to serve the world (I know I do) and can't decide, write them all down first. Then choose the one that resonates most with you right now. The wonderful thing about service is that once you start down that path, you will continue to find new and exciting ways to contribute to making the world around you a better place. You can always come back to your other ideas in the future.

If you can't decide, you can move forward with two ideas for now, and decide during the next stages where you want to focus. You need to decide eventually, though. Many things will change during your application process and study. Your goals might shift. Your professor in Japan could steer you to a different research subject. You might find a whole new area of research that excites you. That's all fine. But once you decide your theme, how you want to serve the world, that should not change.

Next, we're going to work on taking that general theme and breaking it down into specific actions and results.

Going from Theme to Goal:

Goal Brainstorm

Once you have decided on your theme, it's time to brainstorm as many specific ways to contribute to your theme as possible.

You can make a list (there is space in the worksheet for this), draw a web that branches out from general to specific, attack a whiteboard with a marker, whatever works best for you in getting as many ideas as possible out of your head and into writing. Remember, writing is powerful.

Do not censor yourself at this stage or reject any ideas. Write them all out as they come to you. You never know when something that might sound stupid could be the seed of another, better idea. Keep them all as visual cues.

Stop reading and spend at least 10 minutes to do this before you pick up the book again. Keep going until you run out of ideas, then force yourself to come up with five more. Often, it's only after we think we have exhausted every avenue that our brains get creative and come up with the best concepts.

Next, we are going to review how to narrow down your list, but I don't want you thinking about that process yet and limiting your brainstorming.

Narrowing Down Your List

You have your brainstorm list, right?

Good. Because now it's time to whittle that list down to something that you can use to steer your application.

I recommend making a copy of your list to work on. As you eliminate ideas, cross them out, but don't obliterate them. You may want to go back to them or build on them later.

The first thing you want to do is eliminate anything that you could accomplish right now, without earning a graduate degree. Your goal is must connect to your research. If it's something you can already accomplish, then you could start working on that right away instead of going to graduate school first.

Graduate school is about conducting independent, original research. It is not about applying existing research, except for some cases in engineering fields, but even then, you would conduct original experiments. You should be looking for goals that you do not yet have the required knowledge to pursue.

Next, you'll want to look for goals that are out of your control, require resources you can not get access to (yet), or are ideas that you could not start working on for over five years after your graduation. Do **not** eliminate these goals. Instead, try to create an interim goal that will help you on the way to each one: find something that is within your power and is something you can tackle within five years of graduation.

Don't underestimate yourself!

For example, if you had a goal to establish a human settlement on Mars, that's probably not something you can pull off within five years with your resources, unless you happen to be Elon Musk. But it would be a reasonable goal to develop a self-contained mini-farm that could help sustain the growth of plants on Mars.

If you want to restructure tertiary education in your home country to encourage innovation instead of rote learning, that could take a while to accomplish on your own. But your interim goal could be to become a professor at a university in your home country to start that pedagogy change on a grass-roots level and present on your results at academic conferences to influence the change.

Figure out what works best for you and your goals!

Relating to Your Studies

While you are thinking of interim goals—or if you are using one of your brainstormed goals—look for ways to relate the practical goal to what you have studied in the past. The Mars example above works if you have a research background in bioengineering, but what if you have the same Martian goal and a background in literature? In that case, you could contribute to establishing a Mars settlement by identifying common themes in space colonization literature across cultures so that you could use the results of your research to inspire public awareness and enthusiasm for settling Mars.

If you cannot find any way to relate a goal on your list to your past research experience, then eliminate it for now. You can always come back if you figure it out later.

Results

Hopefully, by now, you have three to five goals remaining that excite you, are related to your past research and future goals, and are reasonably achievable within five years of graduation. Write them down on a separate list.

Validating and Revising Your Potential Goals

Now that you have several potential goals that serve your application theme, it's time to validate and revise.

The clearer and more focused you are on your goal, the better you will be able to narrow down your research question for your Field of Study and Research Program Plan. You will have an easier time selecting what university or universities to apply to and professors that you want to work with, since you know your ultimate goal. And you will come across as more focused, confident, and promising throughout your application process.

Before we get started on your goal, let's look at what makes "bad" goals. A "bad" goal is not a goal to do something bad. You don't need to be Ernst Stavro Blofeld or Lord Voldemort to have bad goals.

A bad goal is unfocused, vague, or short-sighted. It doesn't give you enough information or guidance to move forward and make decisions.

Once we've gone through a few bad goals, we'll look at the SMART goal-setting framework and make sure that your final goal statement for your application meets that framework.

What Makes a Bad Goal

There are many ways to write a bad goal, but the most common I see among MEXT applicants is this one:

They look no further than winning the scholarship.

I have people write to me to say that they want the MEXT scholarship because the quality of education in Japan is better, so they will be able to contribute more to their society after graduation.

No good.

Others write they want to increase their chances of employment.

Even worse.

Some applicants respect Japanese culture and want to spend more time surrounded by and experiencing that culture on a daily basis.

Passive and terrible.

These "goals" focus only on the applicants' personal gain, and all would be accomplished simply by winning the scholarship and finishing the associated degrees. These goals show no promise for the future or sign that the applicant will ever contribute to the world in a meaningful enough way to validate the Japanese government's investment.

Remember, the MEXT Scholarship is not a handout or a charity. It is not based on financial need. It is the Japanese government investing in creating future leaders with a connection to Japan. Your goal should show the return on investment that you propose to become.

Another way you can go wrong is by being too vague.

I have had applicants write to say that they want the MEXT scholarship so that they can contribute to world peace.

Sorry, but your winning the scholarship does not make the world a more peaceful place. I think we can all agree that world peace would be a good thing, but this "goal" fails because it is too vague and there is no clear path. As I mentioned above, contributing to peace between nations can be a theme, but it is not specific enough to be a goal.

Another well-meaning but deficient goal is: I want to contribute to my home country.

Great! How? There is no specificity here, either.

As you set your goals, make sure that they serve others and that they meet the SMART goals framework that we will discuss next.

Goals with a History of Success

Remember that your application theme should be about service to others. There are a few common goals that are related to service, are desirable outcomes to MEXT, and have a history of success, particularly among applicants from developing countries:

- Becoming a professor to disseminate the knowledge you gained in Japan to future generations in order to strengthen a field where your country is behind Japan.

- Becoming a government employee with responsibility over policy decisions, where you will use your knowledge and experience in Japan.

However, it is not enough just to say that you want to become a professor or public servant. You will still need to come up with a specific field of research that you want to spread in your home country, along with a reason or a specific field of policy that you want to tackle. But these are both tried-and-true goals that can help you shape an application.

Even if you don't want to become a professor or a bureaucrat, there are endless possibilities for success, so do not be discouraged.

You can find successful applicants from the past who have shared their research proposals and, more importantly, their thinking and planning behind them. Adopting their research ideas wholesale is never a good idea, but understanding their thought process and what went into their planning can help you create strong goals and a winning field of study and research program plan. In introduce some examples in Book 2 of this series: *How to Write a Scholarship-Winning Field of Study and Research Program Plan*. You can find that book at the link below.

https://mymext.com/getmms2

SMART Goals

Now that you understand what to avoid, and a few clear paths, it's time to focus on how to write goals that will drive you toward success. These are the kinds of goals that will give focus to your research plan, help you come across as being confident and competent, and set you apart from unfocused applicants.

The best goal-setting framework I have come across is SMART goals. This is the system that successful entrepreneurs and business coaches use. I know this is a scholarship application, not a business. The goal structure has nothing to do with business and everything to do with success. Entrepreneurs are the most success-driven people out there, since their livelihood depends on achieving their goals, so that's who we want to emulate.

As you have probably guessed, "SMART goals" is an acronym. For now, we are going to go through what each letter means and how it applies to you. You do not need to create your goal from start to finish yet. We will do that in the next few sections and in the worksheet. For now, it's important just to understand the final objective.

- **S - Specific:** What exactly do you want to achieve? Where? When? How? Why? The more details you know about your goal, the stronger your focus and the easier it will be to achieve, since you won't get lost or confused. (We've already covered the "why" with your application theme, so you've got a head start!)

- **M - Measurable:** How will you be able to tell if you are making progress toward your goal or achieve it? Since we're talking about a goal that you want to achieve after graduation, and so much might change before then, you do not need to commit to specific measurements or objectives yet. But you need to think about how you will measure your goals.

- **A - Attainable:** Do you have the resources, or the ability to obtain the resources, to achieve your goal? Is it possible within a set amount of time? Most importantly, are you willing to make the personal sacrifices necessary to achieve it? This is a significant difference between your application theme, which is a cause you want to contribute to, and your goal, which should be a concrete, attainable outcome. You want to push yourself - remember, if your goal is something you can already achieve now, then you won't be able to use it to justify your scholarship application - but don't break yourself or set yourself up for failure.

- **R - Relevant:** Is achieving this goal something that is important to you? Is it something you really want, or something you think others want from you? I have found with my work with students over the years that many who break down during their studies are ones that are following their parents' dreams, not their own. Their dad is a doctor and pushed them to follow the same path, or their career counselor pushed them to go into computer programming for the money. These students, though many were brilliant, struggled and often changed direction, losing time and money. Make sure your goals apply to what you want for yourself.

- **T - Time-bound:** Parkinson's Law states that work expands or contracts to fit the time allowed. If you set yourself a goal but don't put a deadline on it, you will lose focus, slow down progress, and risk never completing it. For your application goal, I recommend setting a goal that you plan to achieve within five years. This might affect what you consider Attainable during that time, so these two criteria need to go hand-in-hand. When you write your Field of Study and Research Program Plan, you will need a specific timeline for your research goals, too, so this is great practice!

I realize all of that can sound a little overwhelming as we get started. You haven't even started your studies yet. So it might sound ridiculous to be setting a goal for 5 years later, based on the assumption that your studies will go as planned.

Yes, that's true. The goal you set now will change. So will your research plan. That's not a problem.

The point of writing goals now is not to commit absolutely to achieving them. The point is to give you direction and focus on creating your application and to show the application reviewers that you can set goals and pursing them on your own. Displaying that skill for the sake of the application process is more important now than the actual goals, which can and should develop over the course of your studies.

For now, it's time to figure out a goal that appeals to you and will help you in the process of choosing your research question and selecting universities in Japan.

Crafting Your Goals

The SMART goal framework is in an easy-to-remember order, but it doesn't always make sense to tackle the elements in that order. If you already have a strong focus, then you can address each letter in the order that you prefer. But most people who come to me asking for advice haven't even yet decided what they want to study, so we're going to start with that assumption.

We will start with R: Relevant. In this first step, we'll make sure your goal ideas from the earlier brainstorm list are important to you, personally, and something you are motivated to achieve.

Next, we will revisit T: Time-bound. We have touched on this before with the five-year assumption, but we will get more clear on your specific situation.

Next, we will move on to S: Specific. You'll decide on something specific that you want to achieve within the five years, including the what, where, and how. (We've already nailed when and why with the previous steps!)

This is most likely going to be the most significant and most challenging step, so it's OK if this takes you a little time to get through.

Once you have your specific goal, you will make sure it is A: Attainable. Finally, you will come up with ways that it could be M: Measurable.

As always, the worksheet is here to help you along the way and the good news is that you have two letters almost complete!

Relevant: How do Your Studies Serve Your Purpose

Look back at your application theme. Is this truly something that *you* want to do? Make sure your theme is not something that others have forced on you or pressured you into accepting. Hopefully, by this time, that is not a problem.

Now, look at the rough goals you brainstormed earlier. You should still have a few left on this list at this point. Focusing on relevance to what you want for yourself in life, choose the one that is most valuable and exciting to you.

This might sound a little selfish, but if you wrote all of your goals from the perspective of serving the world around you, then there is nothing selfish about choosing between different ways to serve. In any life of service, it is critical that your goals be relevant and personal to you. Your internal motivation to pursue your goals will help you get through challenges even when the rest of the world doesn't seem to care.

Any successful service must be underpinned by a personal, intrinsic desire or passion to see it through for your own benefit. This is not selfishness, it is essential to your success.

Go back to your list and circle the goal that you are most passionate about.

Now, write one to two sentences describing why you are passionate about achieving this goal. In your application form and your Field of Study and Research Program Plan and when you take part in the interviews, you will need to explain why your research and post-research goals are important to you. So, these few sentences are a first draft of an explanation that you will use in your application!

Now, you should have your application theme, a rough goal, and a statement of why achieving that goal is important to you!

It's time to put some clear definitions on that goal.

Time-Bound: A Clear End Point

As I mentioned earlier, we're going to assume a five-year period after graduation, so T - Time-bound is already covered. Of course, you may have goals that are longer term and grander than what you can achieve in five years. That's great! But even five years (plus your study time) is a long way out and plenty can change in that time. We'll work on setting a SMART goal in that five-year period that will serve your longer-term goals.

That will also help you articulate to the MEXT scholarship reviewers how you plan to make an immediate impact.

If you're concerned with five years being too long and potential changes, remember this is not set in stone. The purpose of this goal is to shape your application strategy, not to commit you to a result.

Take a minute, too, to ensure that your schedule is realistic. If your goal involves sequential steps, make sure you have allotted enough time for each step. Consider breaking larger goals into smaller ones and setting a Time-Bound deadline for each of the sequential steps you need to make toward your long-term goal!

Specific: Going From Rough Goal to Defined

Going from a rough goal to a specific one might take some time. I don't recommend that you sit down and try to solve this all at once. You might need to go for a walk or sleep on it partway through.

You'll come back to revise this step again as we continue to develop your application strategy. You don't need to get it perfect on the first go around. We will validate the specifics as we consider the Attainable and Measurable criteria. We will also likely need to reshape your goal when we "MEXTify" it in the next section to connect it to specific research and to Japan.

Consider this your "Specific" first draft. You can always change these details later, but first you need to have something to change.

At this point, you have your application theme, which is how you want to serve the world. You have a list of several goals that serve that theme, including one that you have circled as the most Relevant to you. You have also established why that goal is important to you.

Now, we are going to give that goal some shape. We are going to answer:

- **What** outcome you want to achieve because of your studies in Japan.

- **Where** you will take action and achieve this outcome.

- **When** you will plan to achieve the outcome.

- **How** you will achieve the outcome.

- **Why** this outcome serves your application theme.

Let's break down each of those questions.

What

When answering "what" you want to achieve, this should be an outcome that you have the power to accomplish on your own. It should not depend on outside feedback or appraisal that you cannot control.

For example, I once worked on rural rehabilitation projects in a war zone in southeast Afghanistan. One of our missions was to improve the availability of education. So, we had a specific goal to construct at least one boys' school and one girls' school in each of the major towns of our province. Our "what" was to build the schools. That was under our control. We did not set a goal to have X number of female students attending the school, for example, because we could not force parents to send their daughters to school, especially since we were still in a contested area that was largely under Taliban control. (This was before the Taliban took over the country and banned all education for females, but that just highlights the challenges we were up against.)

If we had based our goal on getting a certain number of students, that would have been beyond our control, so it would not have been good enough for a SMART goal.

Your outcome should be within your control, even if you need help to achieve it. If you want to introduce a new technology, then your goal could be to create a proof of concept, but you should not set a goal based on adoption rates. If you want to go into government service and affect policy decisions, then your goal should be to write proposals and lobby politicians or public groups for support, not to guarantee their implementation.

Adoption rates (or school attendance rates, in my case) can and should be goals you go after later, but remember your time constraints and focus on outcomes that are related to your research, for now. Developing a proof of concept is a technological task and one that would be appropriate for a science or engineering degree. Encouraging adoption is a marketing task and would fall under an MBA.

Where

Where are you going to have your impact?

In general, MEXT wants to see you working in your home country. They want graduates to return to their home countries to become a bridge that strengthens relations between that country and Japan.

However, maybe your goal requires that you be working in Japan to develop a specific technology or political initiative that will help your home country and strengthen relations. That could be possible, but the impact area is still your home country, in that case.

Of course, your impact area could be more specific. Maybe you are interested in urban planning and disaster preparedness for a specific city, for land management in a specific national park, or to become a professor at a specific university. Those are all valid "where"s, as well!

When

Earlier, I encouraged you to set your goal within five years of completing your degree. That is for the sake of focus. A task that will take you over five years is likely to be based on multiple cross-supporting initiatives. I wanted you to choose one.

But you don't have to stick to five years as your target. If your goal will or should take less time, be specific about it. Consider how you might have to work with calendar events. Is your goal related to seasons of the year? Is there a specific deadline?

How

How are you going to achieve the outcome you specified under "what"?

You don't need to go into too much detail here—this is only a goal statement, not a complete plan—but you need to be clear about the general activity you need to complete to achieve your outcome.

Why

This statement links your "what" to your application theme. What greater purpose does your outcome serve?

You should already know this, but be sure to include it in your statement.

Example

Taking my schools example above, here's a statement that covers all aspects of the "Specific" criteria:

I will construct one boys' school and one girls' elementary school in the city of Qalat, Afghanistan, prior to the start of the 2030 school year, in cooperation with local officials and construction companies and with financing from USAID, to support the availability of education to all families for the next generation of citizens and improve functioning government and civil society.

Breaking this down, here are the elements:

- What: Build one boys' school and one girls' elementary school

- Where: In the city of Qalat, Afghanistan

- When: Prior to the start of the 2030 school year

- How: In cooperation with local officials and construction companies and with financing from USAID

- Why: To support the availability of education to all families for the next generation of citizens and improve functioning government and civil society

The point of this example is to show a complete goal statement, even though current circumstances make the goal itself impossible. Besides being specific, this goals statement is also Measurable (two schools), Attainable (assuming I was still working in rural rehabilitation in Afghanistan), Relevant (there are few things more important to me, personally, than contributing to the availability of education opportunities), and Time-Bound (2030 school year).

Of course, this specific example is not a good proposal for the MEXT scholarship, because nothing about this goal requires further research. We'll look into shaping goal statements to be appropriate for the MEXT scholarship a little later on.

Attainable: Reality Check

Look back at your goal statement that we wrote in the "Specific" section and decide: Is this really something possible?

You should have written what you want to accomplish and how. If you need external support, especially funding or cooperation, is it within your means to obtain? Is your goal something that global conditions will allow?

Using the worksheet, write out what you need from other people to achieve your goal, and how you plan to get it.

My sample goal of building schools was obtainable for me when I was working in Afghanistan in 2009, because I was part of a NATO team and had access to all the people and resources I needed. Now, it would not be attainable because I have left that world and the Taliban has taken over.

You should also consider obstacles that might make your goal not Attainable. Is there potential political resistance to your idea? Are there physical or logistical obstacles if your goal involves working in remote or difficult areas? Does your goal rely on technology that is not commonly available or not affordable?

For each obstacle you consider, write out a way to overcome it, or change your goal to avoid the obstacle.

Your goal should be ambitious, but if you are not confident that it is even possible to attain, then consider scaling it back. You can always set a new goal once you have hit the first!

You may also have to defend the attainability of your goal during the MEXT Scholarship interview stage. If you set a goal that is unrealistic, or if you cannot make a logical argument about how it would be possible, then scale back to something you can explain. It will not look good to the committee if your goal sounds like an unrealistic pipe dream.

Measurable: Ensuring Quantifiability

If it isn't measured, it isn't done.

Your goal should have an objective measurement. You need to know when you have met the goal and you also need to track your progress along the way.

In the previous example, my goal was to build two schools. That is something I can measure and also something I can track by looking at the construction progress of each school throughout the life of the goal.

Your goal will probably be more difficult to measure. Try to think of ways you can measure your output if you are producing either physical products or intellectual products like policy proposals, software programs, works of art, etc. If your goal involves developing a new technology, then you can measure your progress toward achieving completion, testing, patenting, production, etc.

Your goal statement is going to be one (long) sentence and you do not need to go into too much detail, but know what aspect of the goal you will measure and how you will know how close you are to completion.

Your SMART Goal

By now, you should have a SMART goal drafted in your worksheet. Congratulations! That's a great first step.

But you might be looking at your goal and asking yourself, how does this relate to my application for a graduate degree?

Remember, this goal is what you want to accomplish after your degree. So, your studies in Japan must get you to where you can start work on it. Later, when we discuss your Field of Study and Research Program Plan in Book 2, we will create a separate research goal for your studies.

In the next section, we will walk through the process of making sure that your goal connects to a research program to be conducted in Japan.

MEXTifying Your Goal

Connecting it to Your Studies in Japan

We've reviewed the SMART Goals framework, which is the best approach to setting clear, attainable goals to push you forward. But that is a general framework. In order to make sure that your goals are appropriate for the MEXT scholarship application, we have a few more steps.

In the next sections, we are going to make sure that your goal is related to graduate studies, that it is connected to Japan, and that it strengthens connections between Japan and your home country.

Research Connection

For your goal to be relevant to the MEXT Scholarship application, it *must* require you to conduct original research.

If you already have all the knowledge you need to get working on your goal, then you can't use it as justification to apply for a graduate degree. You could just go get started now. You must need some additional knowledge to be able to complete your goal.

This knowledge can be anything from a more detailed mastery of specific techniques or technologies, to a deeper understanding of case studies and examples than what is available, or new research into specific local conditions.

Remember, all graduate degrees in Japan are research degrees. There is no such thing as a "taught master's", where you just take courses and absorb information. You will be expected to research primary sources to draw new conclusions, conduct experiments, and/or conduct your own field research (in Japan). One of those activities, and its results, must be necessary for your goal.

Even if you are in a professional degree, like an MBA, or a fine arts degree, there will still be a final output to your studies. It might not be the same academic research output as an academic degree, but there should be some final output to your studies to demonstrate your learning and development. Research your specific degree program to figure out what that is, then relate that final output to your goal.

Here are a few examples:

If you are in humanities and social sciences, consider how research of primary sources in Japan can help you develop the knowledge you need to tackle a problem. For example, researching a particular event in Japanese history to apply a greater understanding of the relationship between contemporary conditions and individuals' actions to the outcome to a similar decision point or problem in your home country.

Social science and humanities scholars should also consider how fieldwork in Japan can connect to their goal. Can studying Japanese society through surveys, interviews, etc., help you better understand a particular social issue (such as aging society) to implement social programs in your home country?

In sciences and engineering, your goal statement should depend on developing new technology and systems or adapting technology/systems to conditions in your home country.

Fine arts scholars' goals should require studying from Japanese masters in their fields to merge the understanding of their techniques and philosophies with previous knowledge to create new ideas in arts.

How does this apply to you? Write out what research, new knowledge, or new abilities you require to achieve your goals. If your goal statement does not require any new research or understanding, then you should consider either forgoing the MEXT scholarship to get started on your goal right away or revising that goal statement to establish an obvious need for research before you can start.

Why is Japan the Best Place for Your Studies?

During the application process, you will need to establish a connection between your goal and Japan. If you apply for the Embassy-Recommended MEXT Scholarship, there is an essay question where you have to explain why you chose to study in Japan.

Saying that you want to study in Japan because you grew up addicted to manga and anime will not impress the review committee, unless your research is related to those art forms. So, you'll need a stronger reason. Many applicants also make the mistake of simply praising Japan, its society and culture, or its state of development. That is also weak and irrelevant.

There are several proven reasons that will establish the connection beyond a doubt. Associating one of these with your goal and your research will give you a stronger case for why you must conduct your research in Japan. These are in no particular order. Any of them would be solid reasons.

- You want to conduct field research on a specific incident, case study, or region of Japan to apply that knowledge to your home country.

- Cutting edge research in your field is being conducted in Japan.

- Japan—or even better, a particular university—offers access to unique research resources, such as a particular lab or experiment.

- You have already established a relationship with a professor in Japan based on your research and want to continue to work with them.

- Japan has a unique perspective on your field of study that you cannot explore elsewhere.

- Your post-graduation goal involves working with Japanese companies or organizations in your home country, such as JICA development projects.

- There is a compelling reason you need to establish a research network with Japanese universities or professors that you will continue to leverage, and offer benefit to, after graduation.

As a few of these examples suggest, you don't have to focus on Japan as a whole. If you can make a case for why you must conduct your research at *a specific university in Japan*, that is even stronger, for our purposes. Remember, the point of your goal statement is to give you a clear focus, so that you can wrap your entire application around a central theme and impress the reviewers with your organization and preparation. Clearer is better.

Avoid selfish or short-sighted reasons, such as "because Japan offers a generous scholarship". Even flattering reasons like saying that you respect Japanese culture and society and want to experience it will not be compelling. It is in your best interest to have a practical connection between your goal and research and Japan.

Even if you had not thought of these reasons when starting your application strategy, work one into your plan now. This might require revising your specific goal to consider a field of study where Japan is more advanced. It may also require looking for an example of a case study in Japan that you can apply to your goal.

Even if it takes some time, it is worth the effort to make your application appear that much more organized and focused!

How Does Your Goal Serve the Relationship Between Japan and Your Home Country

Besides thinking about why you must conduct your research in Japan, you need to have an idea about how it will benefit Japan.

The goal of the MEXT Scholarship, from the Japanese government's perspective, is to create connections between rising leaders in countries around the world and Japan. They want you to go home, contribute to your society, and share how Japan helped you get to where you could make that contribution.

If you're applying for Embassy-Recommended MEXT Scholarship, then it is likely that your review committee will include local academics or government bureaucrats from your home country, as well. These people will also have a vested interest in how you will return to help develop your home country and strengthen the connection with Japan.

Many times, it is enough to explain how you will leverage the knowledge and experience you gained in Japan to benefit your home country through your efforts, with specific examples related to your research, and that you will actively advocate for others in your field to study in Japan or work with Japan in the future. Sharing what you learned or experienced in Japan will appeal to the review committee.

This approach works especially well if you plan to go into teaching, but can also work in any practical development field or government service.

Maintaining research relationships with Japan after returning home and exchanging knowledge with your connections in Japan is also a strong connection. It is one of MEXT's explicit goals for the scholarship to expand research networks of Japanese universities overseas.

Remember, too, that one of the unmeasurable eligibility criteria is that you must be willing to participate in follow-up surveys and events conducted by the Japanese Embassy in your home country to promote Japanese culture. If your research is related to Japanese culture, such as in humanities fields, then you could propose that you will spread that knowledge through seminars, exhibitions, or events. You'll want to be more specific to your field, of course.

Even in other fields, including technical fields, proposing to give presentations at local universities, which could inspire more interest in studies or research collaboration in Japan, would also be beneficial.

If you can connect any of those activities to promoting your goal, that is excellent.

In the worst-case scenario, even if there is no obvious direct connection to the attainment of your goal, you should at least be prepared to explain how you plan to advocate for study in Japan to others in your field in order to strengthen human capital in that area, which will further multiply the results of your efforts.

Your SMART Goal, MEXTified

At this point, you should have established a SMART goal that has a clear relationship with Japan.

That puts you ahead of the vast majority of applicants for the scholarship! If you get nothing else out of this book—even if you do not read any other books in this series—you already have a tremendous advantage.

As you complete each of your MEXT application documents and prepare for your interview, keep this goal statement in front of you at all times. When you are considering what to say, whether to include something, or how to explain a particular experience or motivation, relate it back to this goal.

If you do this, you will come across as being organized, reliable, focused, and a strong candidate for the scholarship. The reviewers will see you as someone who can fulfill their objectives after graduation and contribute to Japan and the world.

This is an enormous step, but we are not finished.

Your scholarship application does not exist in a vacuum. It is not just a matter of being "good enough" to earn the scholarship. This is a competition. And like any competition, you need to know the rules and your opposition.

As the next part of preparing your application strategy, we will look at those rules and try to gain a better understanding of the "opposition" and obstacles you may face, as well as how you can prepare to overcome them.

Think About Your "Opposition"

> "If you know your enemy and know yourself, then
> in a thousand battles you need not fear defeat."
> - Sun Tzu

Yes, I know that Sun Tzu is not Japanese. But this quote applies to any endeavor, even if it is too often misunderstood.

The misinterpretation is usually based on the word "enemy." If I say "enemy" to you in the context of the MEXT scholarship application, you might assume I mean the other applicants who are competing for the same scholarship places. But that's not what I mean.

I prefer the word "opposition." Opposition is less negative and more clearly refers to anything that resists your efforts to achieve your goal. An enemy is someone you fight against. Opposition is something that you overcome.

For the MEXT scholarship, other applicants are not your only opposition. Your opposition includes the application process itself, as well as the embassy- and university-level reviewers. You will go head-to-head with the application process, especially trying to understand the complicated requirements, confusing instructions, and unclear expectations. Your application documents, and you, yourself, will undergo scrutiny by reviewers who are looking to eliminate candidates.

This is your opposition and what you need to understand.

Fortunately, you have this book, plus books 2 and 3 in this series, which will help you understand and excel in the key stages of the application process.

As you plan your application strategy, you need to consider the application process from the perspective of the reviewers. Before you submit a document, send an email, or take part in an interview, stop and think about the person on the other end. What does that person want? How can you create an outcome that meets that person's wants and your own?

Consider What's in it for the Other Person at All Times

The best resource I have ever encountered on understanding other people's wants and persuading them to your point of view is Dale Carnegie's book, *How to Win Friends and Influence People*. I recommend the book and you can often find the ebook for cheap prices on Amazon. You can find a link in the resources at the end of this book.

I cannot summarize the entire *How to Win Friends and Influence People* in these few brief paragraphs, but I will highlight the most important points for MEXT applicants.

Your task is to understand what your opposition (MEXT, your reviewers) wants and phrase your own goals in such a way that they match what the opposition wants.

MEXT and the Embassy

MEXT wants you to become a leader in your home country and a cultural ambassador for Japan throughout your career.

Becoming a leader does not mean that you have to become president. You can be a leader in government service, but you can also be a leader in academia as a professor or administrator, a leader in industry, a leader of a community, or a leader of a social or cultural movement.

Of course, it will take more than the five years we set previously to reach a leadership position, but your first goal should be a concrete step along that path.

From that position of leadership, as small or large as it may be, consider how you can be an ambassador for Japanese culture. We covered this earlier, but it bears reiterating, when you state your post-MEXT studies goal in the Field of Study and Research Program Plan and describe it in your interview, make every effort to connect it to your role as an informal ambassador for Japan and contributor to relationships between Japan and your home country.

Your Government

If your government is involved in the selection process during the Embassy-Recommended MEXT Scholarship, you will need to emphasize how your goal serves your people or your home country in a meaningful way.

Your Target Advisor in Japan

When you build a relationship with your target advising professor in Japan, follow the basic tenets of any networking effort: Offer value.

Unlike the embassy and government staff, who may be concerned more with what you will do after graduation, university professors in Japan will be more interested in your research goals and how that could offer value to the professor's own research and field of study.

You should learn all you can about each target professor's current research and initiatives before contacting them and describe your own research goals in relation to how they compliment your target advisors'.

In science and engineering fields, you will often have to work on a specific research project that your professor needs done, especially at the PhD level.

In humanities and arts (fine and liberal), you may not be working directly on a sub-theme of your professor's research, but you will help to broaden the scope of research within their field.

Of course, in any field, a goal to publish and/or go on into academia yourself also benefits your advisor by increasing his or her stature in the field.

You do not need to be obsequious or volunteer yourself as a professor's slave. Avoid that. Present yourself as someone who desires to become a peer and long-term research connection, and you will put yourself on a path to a stronger long-term relationship.

What Will Help and Hurt Your Chances

Two of the most common questions I have seen over the years on my blog have been:

- "Will X help my chances of winning the scholarship?"

- "Will Y hurt my chances of winning the scholarship?"

Applicants ask if experience studying abroad in Japan will help them, or if never having left their country will hurt them. Will some Japanese language ability help? What about being a research assistant or the president of a university manga club?

After reading the last several sections, you may already realize what is wrong with these questions.

Other applicants have more practical, but still misguided questions, like asking whether applying for the same level degree that they have already earned will hurt them.

You'll hear this answer a *lot* once you win the scholarship and arrive in Japan: It depends.

The "So What?" Factor

The problem with the questions above is that they refer only to isolated facts. They are missing the "so what?" factor that gives them significance. Over the last several sections of this book, we have gone over goals and building your application around a central theme. Facts will not help or hurt you unless you give them meaning and connect them to your goal.

The right questions to ask are:

- *"How* can I use X to help my chances of winning the scholarship?"

- *"How* can I mitigate the damage to my application from Y?"

Over the next few sections, we look at the kinds of experiences and abilities that can be helpful, help you find examples in your own life, and, most importantly, figure out how you can leverage those facts for maximum benefit to your application.

What Are Your Superpowers

You have superpowers.

I don't mean that you can fly, read minds, or shoot laser beams out of your nose.

I mean that there is *something* you do better than most people around you. There is some unique experience, background, passion, or combination that you bring to the table that no other applicant does. We have to identify what that is.

You don't have to be the best in the world at whatever your superpower is. Chances are good that your superpower is a combination of things: A particular background, plus experience, plus passion in a field, plus an ability. That combination—your story—makes you unique and you can use that uniqueness as an advantage.

What Are You Good At?

I've said this before, but it bears repeating: I know only one thing about you for sure. I know you are the type of person who invests in yourself and your goals. You didn't just approach the MEXT scholarship application with the attitude of "Well, I'll give it a shot and hope it works out." You bought a book to study the application process and how to strengthen your application. Chances are, you've also combed through all the free advice and information I've posted on my blog, too, right?

So, I know you are a person who has a thirst for knowledge and who attempts to understand their tasks and goals.

I'm also going to assume that you're a person who puts in the work to make those goals a reality. (You have been filling in the worksheets as we went along, right?)

That is already a significant superpower. You take steps on your own to learn what you need to succeed in your goals and follow through with action to make it a reality. You may take it for granted because it's a trait you possess, but trust me, it's rarer than you think.

So, that's one superpower. It's your turn to come up with more:

- What do you do better than most people around you? (Don't overlook "mundane" abilities like clear communication, time management, or analytical ability!)

- What do other people come to you for help with?

- What are you so passionate about that you would do it all day, even if you weren't getting paid?

- When you work in a group, what task to you usually take on?

(These questions are on the worksheet, so you can fill in your answers there to keep them all together!)

If you're modest or self-effacing, you will fit in well in Japanese society, but you might struggle to complete this list. In that case, ask friends and family what *they* think you are good at and write those things down, as well.

Don't leave anything out, even if it seems irrelevant. Even skills that are not relevant to your goal or your research in Japan may be related to a more fundamental ability that you *can* apply to your application. By listing everything out, you will find common themes and make connections that you wouldn't have realized if you were self-censoring.

For example, I am an excellent baker. My friends and family go crazy for my sweets and breads. That doesn't necessarily sound like it could connect to a research goal, but it is. My skill in baking is based on my ability and dedication to study the recipe, prepare my workspace in advance, measure precisely, implement the correct mixing techniques, and practice, practice, practice, until I get my creations right. Those are all skills that I can apply to research in Japan, even if I never bring a pie into the lab.

Once you have your list of skills, do what I did with the baking example above and extract the relevant parts. Look for characteristics that show up across multiple superpowers. For example, in baking, I mentioned studying the recipe in advance. I have several other superpowers where my success is based on my ability to analyze the task and be prepared in advance, so that is something I would want to connect to my research goal.

Strength of Past Accomplishments

To paraphrase *Hamlet*, there is nothing good or bad, but framing makes it so.

When you list your past accomplishments, you must put them in context. Do not expect your reviewer to make that connection for you or to understand why a particular achievement or experience makes you a stronger candidate for the scholarship.

Whenever you mention your past, whether in the Field of Study and Research Program Plan, during the interview, or communicating with your prospective advisor, be sure to link it to your goals and your understanding of the reviewers' needs.

Some accomplishments have obvious connections, but even in these cases, you should still mention the obvious, even if briefly. Remember, your reviewers are seeing dozens of applications. They are hearing the same things over and over. You need to make your statements stand out by highlighting them with characteristics and results that the reviewers are looking for.

For example, earning top grades is good but inconclusive. Did you earn your grades by choosing easy classes or by working hard? Reviewers don't know. But explaining how you earned those grades, or the lengths you were willing to go to when you struggled and needed to work extra hard, will help show your dedication and will persuade the reviewers that you will overcome the transition to a higher-level degree in a new country.

If you have worked as a research assistant, do not just state the fact, explain that it gave you experience operating an academic lab and ongoing research as well as how it contributed to your passion to further your own studies.

If you have studied abroad in the past, whether in Japan or another country, simply stating that will not help you as much as describing specific examples that show how you grew and how you will apply that experience to your studies in Japan. If you do have study abroad experience, remember that besides your goal and your "opposition's" needs, the reviewers also want to make sure that you can adapt to life in Japan. Leverage this experience to show how you adapted to a new culture and academic system, got involved in the community, and how you will apply that to your MEXT studies.

Use your past achievements and experiences to highlight your unique characteristics and advantages to the review committee and you will gain a significant advantage over the applicants who simply list up their past and expect someone else to make the connection.

Language Proficiency and Professional Certifications

Besides required proficiency in the language of your degree program, you can leverage other language proficiencies or professional proficiencies related to your field of study in some situations.

High proficiency in a particular language, at the native level, for example, gives you access to a broader research network and resources. If you can connect that potential to your research topic, that is another superpower you can leverage in your application.

Even low levels of language proficiency can give you a slight advantage. Having a little proficiency in other languages can tell the review committee that you like to learn about new languages and cultures and make the extra effort to communicate and get involved. Those are desirable traits for MEXT scholars.

Of course, as we just discussed, you need to make sure that you draw that deliberate connection. Don't leave it to the review committee to figure it out on their own. If your language proficiency relates to your research, mention it in your Field of Study and Research Program Plan. If it relates to adapting to new cultures, mention it when questioned about your ability to adapt to life in Japan during your interview or in the context of what you can contribute to the relationship between countries in the Embassy-Recommended MEXT Scholarship application essay.

Professional Certifications

For professional certifications, you only need to focus on qualifications that apply to your goal or studies. Honestly, over three years and well over 500 applications, I never once saw an applicant submit a relevant or useful certification. So, if you don't have one, it is not something you need to worry about.

I used to see applicants submit passing certificates for introductory courses in Microsoft Office use. Nobody cares. That's about as valuable as a certificate saying you have learned how to brush your teeth. Do not submit a certificate just for the sake of submitting one. Make sure they are relevant.

If you have a certification or license related to your field of study that you had to work for, that is something you should bring up. For instance, if you have a veterinary license and are applying for a PhD in life sciences to research animal pathogens, your background is relevant. If you have passed the LEED exam for green architecture, that would apply to an architecture or urban planning degree.

If you have an advanced professional certificate that is *not* related to your field of study, then once again, its value comes down to how well you frame it. You will need to connect that certification to how it has led to your current research interest. If you can show that connection and explain the transition in fields, then you can use that example to prove your dedication to excellence in whatever field you pursue.

I once sat on an interview committee for an office admin job, and one of our applicants was a trained and licensed veterinarian. The job itself had nothing to do with animals, but he explained how he had pursued a career in the veterinary field because of a passion for animals since childhood. But once he started his career, he discovered he had more passion for working with large-scale data analysis, research, and macro solutions to problems than he did for surgery and talking crying children through the death of their beloved dog. He used his story to explain how he pursued excellence in his field, but also recognized his own talents and ability to better serve in another field.

If you cannot connect your past certifications to your current interest, leave those out of your application altogether.

If you do not have any professional certifications, do not worry. It will not put you at any significant disadvantage. But if you do, that is one more tool you can leverage, so try to find the best way to connect your certifications with the goal of your studies!

Japan Experience

Any experience with visiting Japan, interacting with Japanese people, or taking part in Japanese cultural activities is something that you can leverage for the benefit of your application, if you do it right.

There are three primary ways you can leverage your experience with Japan:

- Prove to the review committee that you can adjust to life in Japan

- Show why you are motivated to complete your research in Japan (as we covered earlier)

- Highlight relationships in Japan to show your preparedness and focus

Ability to Adjust to Life in Japan

In the interview, your reviewers are going to want to determine whether you can adjust to life as a graduate scholar in Japan, away from your culture and your support network of family and friends. This is where you can use your experience to ease their concerns and quickly check that box off of their review criteria.

If you have lived in Japan for any length of time, that is a great thing to mention. If not, then experience working with Japanese citizens or exchange students in your home country to help them adjust to life there is also valuable, since it offers an example of how you have already come to understand the cultural differences and helped people to overcome them in the opposite direction.

Experience studying Japanese culture or being part of a Japanese cultural society can also be a useful leverage point. If you took part in tea ceremony or *aikido*, for example, you could talk about how you plan to continue to take part in that once you arrive in Japan and use that experience to build your local connections and adjust. It also shows that you have some experience as a cultural ambassador already.

If your only experience with Japan is growing up watching anime and reading manga, mention it, but I would not suggest that you go into much detail, unless you are researching one of those media. Your reviewers may be wary that you will face culture shock when you learn Japan is nothing like its portrayal in anime or that you have false expectations about the country.

If you do bring up an anime or manga interest, I would recommend that you refer more to the underlying themes or artistic styles, rather than the content.

When you leverage your experience with Japan to show that you can adjust to life in Japan, you are only trying to check off a box. Keep your reference to your experience in Japan short and simple. Use the strongest connection you have to answer their question and keep moving. Stay focused on your goal and your application theme.

Why You Are Motivated to Research in Japan

Earlier, we established why your research had to be completed in Japan. Mentioning experience with Japan or Japanese culture and how that kick-started your interest in your research topic is one way to reinforce that point to your reviewers, show your motivation, and establish a grounding point in Japan.

Preparedness and Focus

If you have study abroad experience at a Japanese university and remain in contact with your faculty members there, you can leverage that when you establish your dedication to your research plan. Showing that you are already in contact with faculty members in Japan about your research and have interest from a professor is going to be a strong mark in your favor.

I will cover building relationships with faculty members in Book 3 of this series, but remember that a relationship built in person while in Japan serves both your research and proof of your preparedness to live in Japan!

Potential Obstacles and Disadvantages

I mentioned at the start of this section that applicants often contact me to ask whether a particular condition or situation will hurt their application. The most common questions I get about disadvantages fall in to the three categories below:

- Applying for the same level of degree that you have already earned in the past

- Long periods of unemployment

- Lack of any intercultural experience

Remember what I said earlier: Asking if something will help or hurt you is the wrong question. If you have any situation that you are concerned might hurt your application, the question you need to ask is, "How can I keep this from hurting my application chances?"

The answer is to justify the situation by connecting it to your goal and application theme. Don't just make excuses for yourself, phrase your explanation as a reason the potential obstacle contributes to your goal.

I will cover the three topics above in more detail, but you can use the same justification approach for any potential obstacle or weakness.

Repeating a Degree Level

If you have already earned a master's degree and want to apply for another master's degree in Japan, you need to justify that decision.

Why is a second master's degree more advantageous to your goal than a PhD would be? What does a master's degree offer you that a doctoral degree does not?

I have never seen an applicant offer a satisfactory answer to this question when continuing in the same field of study. If you are continuing in the same field of study, then there should be nothing a second master's offers that a doctoral degree would not. The only possible justification I have seen is a pivot. If you had earned an MSc and focused on developing a new technology in your research and now want to learn techniques to better distribute that technology, then it could make sense to transition to an MBA. Or perhaps to a field like urban planning or policy science where you could study implementation of your new technology.

Do not justify repeating a degree by saying that you are not academically prepared to move on to the next level. That does not make you look good.

There is one practical consideration to keep in mind, as well. If you are applying to repeat a degree that you have already earned, you could not start as a research student. You would have to start as a degree-seeking student.

Unemployment or Gaps in Your Work/Academic History

Gaps in your academic and work history can look bad on paper, even if there is a legitimate reason for it. Japan is a society where many of the older generation still attach high importance to belonging to an organization. In fact, if someone is mentioned on the news, whether for good or bad reasons, their employment status will almost always be stated. A high proportion of criminal suspects are identified as being unemployed, so there may be an unconscious bias against that status.

I'm not saying that is the right attitude to have, but you should understand that it is a common attitude among the reviewers and prepare yourself. If your academic and work history shows long periods of unemployment, be prepared to explain those in your interview.

Unemployment because you couldn't find work will not look good. But unemployment because you had to focus on supporting your family at home, or because you were conducting self-study or attempting to become an entrepreneur or independent artist are not bad things.

In any of those cases, be prepared to talk about what you did during that period of unemployment and how it motivated your current study interest and goal.

Lack of Intercultural Experience

It is not uncommon for MEXT scholarship applicants to come from areas where they had minimal contact with people from other cultures. There are even regions of Japan where most locals have had no contact with outsiders. Many applicants have asked me in the past whether it will hurt their application chances if they do not have any intercultural experience.

No. I think that even in this situation, you can find an example of a way you have interacted with another "culture" or way of thinking. If you came from a remote area, then even going to university, for example, would be a form of culture shock. Even if all of your classmates were from the same country, they would have been from other regions. Your professors would have different perspectives from your family and friends at home. Talking about how you adjusted to that new university culture, and how you used that experience to learn how to adjust to new ways of thinking, can help you overcome the absence of any international experience.

Your Application Strategy: Conclusion

It's been a long chapter, with a lot of hard thinking and strategizing. But by making it this far, you already have a significant advantage over other MEXT applicants.

You have an application theme, a way to serve the world in the future.

You have a SMART goal that serves that theme, which you will use as the focus of your research plan and interview preparation.

You have connected your SMART goal to a research outcome.

You have justified why your research must be done in Japan.

You have thought through what your reviewers want from you as a MEXT scholar and determined how to phrase your goal so that it meets what they want and expect.

You have listed out your superpowers and experiences that you can use to show why you are a better candidate for the scholarship than anyone else.

Finally, you have considered problems and obstacles that could hold you back and come up with a deliberate plan to overcome them.

That's a ton of work to put in, and I congratulate you on making it through. Now that you have this strategy document in place, keep it in view at all times throughout your application. Print out the worksheets and post them on your wall. Refer to it before you fill in any form, write any email, and prepare for your interview. This focus and strategy will guide you whenever you are concerned about what to do next!

As we say in Japan, *gokurosama deshita* (Thank you for your hard work)!

Exercise 4: Your Application Strategy

The exercises that accompany this chapter are some of the most important in this entire series of books. These questions will help you create your application strategy, from start to finish, and give you a goal-centered approach to the scholarship.

Once you have finished this section, I recommend you print out your answers and post them over your desk, or somewhere else where you can see them every time you sit down to work on your application.

If you are going to be printing these out, then I recommend downloading the document pack if you haven't already done so:

https://mymext.com/bonusmms1

OK, let's get started.

Developing Your Goal

1. In what way do you want to serve the world (What is your application theme)?

2. Brainstorm specific things you could do that would contribute to that theme.

3. Narrow down your brainstorm list to goals that you can accomplish within 5 years that are related to your research background. List your top 3-5 goals, in order of preference.

SMART Goals

4. After reading the section on Relevance, circle the goal from question 3 that you are most passionate about, for your own benefit.

5. In one to two sentences, explain why achieving your goal is important to you. What is in it for you?

6. What exact outcome do you plan to achieve?

7. Where will your outcome's area of impact be?

8. When will you achieve this outcome?

9. How will you go about achieving the outcome?

10. Why does this outcome support your application theme?

11. Write a draft sentence that incorporates the answers to question 6 - 10 in a single goal statement.

12. If your goal requires any sequential steps, write out each step and the deadline for that step to ensure that you meet your overall completion deadline.

13. What external support (funding, cooperation, permission, etc.) does your goal require?

14. For each support you listed in question 13, describe how you plan to secure it, or if it is impossible to secure, write an alternative final goal that will not require that support.

15. What obstacles do you face in your goal? Consider physical, technological, political, and personal obstacles.

16. For each obstacle in question 15, write how you will overcome or avoid it.

17. What specific aspect of your goal will you measure to determine when it is complete (or how close it is to being complete)?

18. If you had to change your end goal because of obstacles or reliance on outside support, rewrite your goal statement with the new final objective.

Why Your Goal Requires Study in Japan

19. How does your goal require additional, original research?

20. If you cannot identify a clear relationship between the need for research and your goal, rewrite your goal statement so that it requires research, knowledge, understanding, or technology that you do not yet have access to, but can acquire during your time in Japan.

21. Why does your research have to be conducted in Japan, or at a particular university in Japan?

22. List all the ways you can think of that your efforts to attain your post-graduation goal could strengthen the relationship between your home country and Japan.

23. List any supporting activities related to your goal that you could do to promote connections between your home country and Japan after graduation.

Considering Your Opposition's Needs

24. How can attaining your goal lead to you becoming a leader in your home country, so that you can be an effective cultural ambassador for Japan? Include the field where you plan to become a leader.

25. (Especially if you are applying for the Embassy recommendation) How does your goal serve your home country?

26. What value does your research plan offer to a potential adviser in Japan?

Your Superpowers

27. What do you do better than most people around you?

28. What do other people come to you for help with?

29. What are you so passionate about that you would do it all day, even if you weren't getting paid?

30. When you work in a group, what task do you usually take on?

31. Ask your friends or family what they think you are good at and write those down, too.

32. What are the common underlying abilities that support each of your superpowers?

Leveraging Your Past

33. What academic experiences do you have (top grades, study abroad, research assistantship, publications, presentations, etc.)? List each experience and at least one way that you can connect that experience to your goal for your MEXT scholarship or to one of your superpowers that will give you an advantage over other applicants.

34. List the languages other than Japanese or English where you have any proficiency and your level (academic, daily conversation, minimal).
34.a. For any academic-level proficiency, how can you use that to serve your research interest in Japan? Are there particular advantages that language offers?
34.b. For daily conversation or minimal proficiency, how can you use that ability to show your adaptability to new cultures and/or willingness to interact?

35. List any professional certifications you have related to your field of study and connect them to your specific research.

36. List any professional certifications you have that are *not* related to your field of study. Is there some way you can leverage them to show your dedication and follow-through ability, while also connecting them to your goal in Japan?

37. What experience do you have with Japanese culture or working with Japanese people? For each one, list the experience and one or two ways that having that experience makes you better prepared to adjust to life in Japan.

38. What, if any, disadvantages or obstacles might hold back your application? For each one, list a justification that connects to your goal.

In Closing

We've come a long way together over the course of this short book. Regardless of how well you understood the MEXT scholarship when you started, you should now be in a position to start your successful scholarship application.

We started with an overview of the MEXT scholarship to help you understand what was possible as well as the purpose of the scholarship, from the Japanese point of view. The first chapter provided the information you need to decide on which scholarship application process to pursue, when to start, and how to apply.

In the next chapter, we discussed the mindset you need for success. I introduced the idea of approaching the scholarship application like a profession, as well as the attitude you need to succeed. That seemingly small change in perspective will help you see the scholarship application process in a new light and can help you with difficult decisions throughout the application process.

Next, we went through the long eligibility checklist. While this chapter might have been boring, it should have cleared up any doubts you had about whether or not you could apply. That's important, because if you are *eligible* to apply, then there is no reason why you cannot succeed with the proper mindset and strategy.

Creating your application strategy was the final and most important chapter of the book. It is one of the most overlooked but important steps of the application. Your strategy will guide your application decisions, help you express yourself more clearly and to the point, and give you a huge advantage over applicants who just put their information out there and hope for the best.

Hopefully, you've downloaded the exercise worksheets and followed along with all of the questions as we went through. If you haven't, I highly recommend that you do that now!

https://mymext.com/bonusmms1

If you have the mindset and your strategy down, then there is no obstacle that you cannot overcome. You will be able to find an answer to any question you might have. You will know to look for advice when you need it, instead of floundering around.

You have invested in yourself by completing the tasks in this book. Carry that attitude forward and there is nothing you cannot do.

What Comes Next?

By now, you should know how to approach the application and whether you will start with the Embassy-Recommended MEXT Scholarship or the University-Recommended MEXT Scholarship. The application timeline will determine your next step. If the application guidelines are available now, you should get started with preparing your application documents. If not, then I recommend that you start working on your Field of Study and Research Program Plan and on researching universities and target advisors in Japan in the meantime.

Field of Study and Research Program Plan

In this book, we covered your overall application strategy and your goals for after graduation. Your research must connect to and serve those goals. The most important tool you have to establish that connection - indeed the single most important document in your application package - is your Field of Study and Research Program Plan.

Writing a concise, effective plan that exceeds the reviewers' expectations is critical to your success. You only have a few pages to make an impression, but this document is so critical, that I recommend you give yourself weeks or months to complete and revise it, then seek feedback to make it better.

In book 2 of the Mastering the MEXT Scholarship series, *How to Write a Scholarship-Winning Field of Study and Research Program Plan,* I walk you through the step-by-step process of determining a research field that meets your goals, writing and validating a research question, and writing the research proposal for submission.

Available now from my store or wherever you usually buy your books or ebooks.

https://mymext.com/getmms2

About the Author

I am a former international student in Japan turned university administrator.

I spent three years working as the first point of contact and reviewer of all MEXT Scholarship applications at a major Japanese private university, where I personally reviewed over 500 Embassy-Recommended MEXT Scholarship and University-Recommended MEXT Scholarship applications and answered thousands of questions.

After moving to another Japanese university, I started researching and writing about the MEXT Scholarship application on my blog, TranSenz, in 2014 and have become the leading independent authority on the scholarship. I have helped thousands of MEXT scholars through the free articles on the blog, this book series, and my coaching service. My goal is to help dedicated and able scholarship applicants overcome confusion about the application process, reduce the role of chance in their success, and realize their dreams of studying in Japan.

I still follow the most recent news and application developments on the MEXT scholarship, as well as within Japanese higher education, in English and Japanese, and share that information with as many people as I can.

Other Books by Travis

Travis writes practical manuals for living in Japan as well as epic fantasy novels.

Mastering the MEXT Scholarship Series

Get a discount on books 2 and 3 when you buy them together directly from me at the link below!

1. *How to Win the MEXT Scholarship*
   https://mymext.com/getmms1

2. *How to Write a Scholarship-Winning Field of Study and Research Program Plan*
   https://mymext.com/getmms2

3. *How to Find your best Degree Program and Advisor for the MEXT Scholarship*
   https://mymext.com/getmms3

Other TranSenz Guides

How to Get a Spouse Visa for Japan: The TranSenz Guide
https://www.transenzjapan.com/svj/

Epic Fantasy Novels (as T.A. Senzaki)

Breyik the Apprentice
https://travissenzaki.com/book/breyik-the-apprentice/

Exercises

If you haven't completed the exercises earlier in the book and want them all in one place, here they are.

As a reminder, you can download these exercises as a worksheet, with space to answer questions, plus a list of all the links and resources in this book from:

https://mymext.com/bonusmms1

Chapter 1: Understanding the MEXT Scholarship

Your Degree

1. What degree do you want to earn by the end of your scholarship? (Master's / PhD / Professional Master's / Professional Doctorate)

2. What is the first degree you need to earn to get there?

3. Do you have a reason that you need to earn your degree quickly and return to your home country (e.g. if you are on a leave of absence from work)?

4. Are you applying to repeat a degree that you have already earned? If so, why?

Your Application Schedule

5. What month is it as you are reading this?

Ideally, you should start preparing for your application about 2-6 months or more before the application deadline. The deadlines should be around May for the Embassy-Recommended MEXT Scholarship or October for the University-Recommended MEXT Scholarship. You can prepare in less time, but it will require significantly more concentrated work.

6. Based on the explanation above, what application process are you going to apply for first? (Embassy / University)

Your Goals and Resources

7. What is your life goal that will benefits from earning the degree above via the MEXT Scholarship? (It can be a broad goal for now, we will refine it later!)

8. What practical resources do you have that you can use to aid your scholarship application?

- Contact with your academic advisor from your last degree

- Contact with a professor in your field in Japan

- A strong relationship with an academic professional who can review your Field of Study

- Access to a university library

- Contact with someone who has won the scholarship in the past

- Contact with a friend or professional who can proof-read your application

- Other

Chapter 2: Successful Applicant Mindset

Confidence

This is an exercise I still use every time I think I don't have what it takes. It always helps me at least to pretend that I have the confidence I need long enough to get the job done.

1. Are you concerned you won't be able to compete for the MEXT scholarship?

2. Why? What disadvantages do you think you have? Be specific.

3. Do you think no other applicant has those same problems or concerns?

4. If every other applicant is human, too, with strengths and weaknesses, what strengths do you have that can set you apart from them? (Here's one: You're a person who invested the time and money in yourself to succeed, as evidenced because you're reading this book and following through with the exercises!)

5. If you apply for the scholarship and don't get it, what's the worst that could happen to you? Again, be specific.

6. So what? Is that worse than what happens if you never apply at all?

Professionalism

7. Imagine *you* were offering an award worth 10,000,000 yen. How would you expect applicants to address you in an email?

8. What characteristics would you look for in their plans?

9. How would you expect applicants to dress and prepare mentally for an interview?

10. On a more practical matter, how often do you check your email and what alerts and systems can you set up to make sure you notice important messages?

Humility

11. Do you think you need any special consideration during the application process? (e.g. no language proficiency scores, financial difficulty in sending materials or traveling to the embassy)

12. What can you do on your own to overcome those challenges?

13. Do you communicate well in writing in English?

14. Is there someone you could ask to test your emails to the embassy and university to make sure your message gets across? Preferably, choose someone who is timely, reliable, and not afraid to give you their frank opinion.

15. Do you immediately asks questions or do you do research on your own? If you tend to ask questions before doing your own searching, what can you do to help yourself overcome that problem?

Chapter 3: Eligibility

1. What is the last degree you earned? Or, if you are still enrolled in a degree program, what level is that degree and when will you finish all of your graduation requirements? Level: / Completion Date:

2. Have you earned, or will you earn, the prerequisite degree before arriving in Japan (Earned a bachelor's degree for master's applicants or a master's degree for doctoral applicants)? Yes / No

Your answer to question 2 must be "Yes" to be eligible.

3. Do you have Japanese nationality? No / Yes
3.a. If yes, are you a dual national and willing to surrender your Japanese nationality? Yes / No

If you answered "Yes" to question 3 and "No" to question 3.a, you are not eligible to apply. Any other combination of answers is eligible.

4. Does your country of nationality have diplomatic relations with Japan? Yes / No

Your answer to question 4 must be "Yes" to be eligible.

5. What year are you applying?
5.a. What calendar year will you start your studies in Japan?
5.b. Subtract 35 from 5.a.
5.c. Is your date of birth on or after April 2 of the year you calculated in 5.b.? Yes / No

Your answer to question 5.c must be "Yes" to be eligible.

6. Do you have any health conditions that require you to stay in your home country for treatment and would prevent you from studying in Japan? No / Yes

Your answer to question 6 must be "No" to be eligible.

7. Do you have language proficiency test scores for the language you plan to study in? Yes / No

7.a. Did you complete (or will you complete) your prerequisite degree in the language of the program in Japan (Japanese or English)? Yes / No

7.b. If you answered "No" to 7 and 7.a. above and you are not a native speaker, when is the next TOEFL iBT/IELTS/JLPT test in your area?

Reference:

- TOEFL iBT Online Portal:
  https://mymext.com/toefl

- IELTS Test Dates and Locations:
  https://mymext.com/ielts

- JLPT Test Dates and Locations:
  https://mymext.com/jlpt

Note: MEXT accepts completion of your prerequisite degree in the same language as proof of language ability, but some universities may not. Check the specific requirements for the universities where you want to study!

8. In what ways could you leverage your research to contribute to the local community (e.g. giving presentations or lessons to community groups, working on specific projects)?

9. Are you willing to get involved in visits to schools and public organizations or volunteer at festivals and events while in Japan? Yes / No

10. Is there any reason (work, school, inability to obtain passport) that you could not leave your home country during the time specified by MEXT to arrive in Japan? No / Yes

Your answer to question 10 must be "No" to be eligible.

11. Have you ever been deported from Japan or left Japan under a Departure Order in the past? No / Yes
11.a. If you answered "Yes" to question 11, you will have a specific period during which you may not reenter Japan. When does that period end?
11.b. Would your studies start after that date? Yes / No

Your answer to question 11 must be "No" or your answer to question 11.b must be "Yes" to be eligible.

12. Are you currently an active-duty member of the military or a civilian employed by the military? No / Yes
12.a. If you answered yes to question 9, are you able to be

discharged or released from your contract before you would start your studies in Japan? Yes / No

Your answer to question 12 must be "No" or your answer to question 12.a must be "Yes" to be eligible.

13. Have you received a MEXT scholarship (other than the Japanese Studies Scholarship, the Japan-Korea Joint Government Scholarship Program For The Students In Science and Engineering Departments, or the Young Leaders Program) in the past? No / Yes

13.a. If you answered "Yes" to question 13, what was the last month when you received a scholarship payment?

13.b. How many complete months of university enrollment or full-time employment do you have since that date, starting with the month after your last payment?

Your answer to question 13 must be "No" or your answer to question 13.b must be "36" or higher to be eligible.

14. (University-Recommended MEXT Scholarship, only) Do you plan to apply to only one university this year via the University-Recommended MEXT Scholarship process, regardless of scholarship category? Yes / No

Your answer to question 14 must be "Yes" to be eligible.

15. Do you have any ongoing MEXT Scholarship application for which you have not received your final results (e.g. previous year's application or ongoing Embassy-Recommended

MEXT Scholarship application)? Yes / No / I applied but was rejected (did not pass one of the screenings)

If your answer to question 15 is "Yes", you will not be eligible to apply again until the results of the current application are final.

16. Are you enrolled in a Japanese university or other institution and residing in Japan with a "Student" residence status? No / Yes

16.a. If you answered "Yes" to question 16, will you graduate and return to your home country before the start of the degree program that you are applying to via the MEXT scholarship? Yes / No

Your answer to question 16 must be "No" or your answer to question 16.a must be "Yes" to be eligible.

17. Do you plan to enroll in a Japanese university or other institution in Japan as a self-financed student and reside in the country with a "Student" residence status between the time you apply for the MEXT scholarship and when you arrive in Japan to start your scholarship-funded studies? No / Yes

Your answer to question 17 must be "No" to be eligible.

18. (University-Recommended MEXT Scholarship, General Category, only) Are you residing in Japan with a residence status other than "Temporary Visitor"? No / Yes

Your answer to question 18 must be "No" to be eligible.

19. Are you applying for or have you been selected for any other scholarships from the Japanese government that will provide money for tuition, living expenses, travel costs to Japan, etc., during your time as a MEXT scholar? No / Yes

If you answered "Yes" to question 19, you must be prepared to cancel your application or withdraw from the award for any other scholarships. (But not for grants for specific projects, etc.)

20. Does your research plan require you to conduct field research or take part in an internship outside of Japan? No / Yes

Your answer to question 20 must be "No" to be eligible.

21. Do you plan to take a leave of absence at any time during your studies? No / Yes

Your answer to question 21 must be "No" to be eligible.

22. Is it your intention to earn a degree (at least) from a Japanese university as a MEXT scholar? Yes / No

Your answer to question 22 must be "Yes" to be eligible.

23. Describe how your intended field of study in Japan is related to your major or to research you have already conducted at university.

24. Write the name of at least one university in Japan that teaches your field of study at the degree level you want in a

language you are qualified to speak. You can find information about how to search for programs taught in English at the link below:

https://mymext.com/professors

25. Does your research concern materials or technology that could be used for the development or production of weapons of mass destruction? No / Yes

Your answer to question 25 must be "No" to be eligible.

26. Calculate your GPA using the My MEXT Scholarship GPA Spreadsheet (or by hand). You can download the spreadsheet from:

https://mymext.com/bonusmms1

What is your GPA (maximum 2 decimal places)?

Your answer to question 26 must be 2.30 or higher to be eligible.

Chapter 4: Your Application Strategy

Developing Your Goal

1. In what way do you want to serve the world (What is your application theme)?

2. Brainstorm specific things you could do that would contribute to that theme.

3. Narrow down your brainstorm list to goals that you can accomplish within 5 years that are related to your research background. List your top 3-5 goals, in order of preference.

SMART Goals

4. After reading the section on Relevance, circle the goal from question 3 that you are most passionate about, for your own benefit.

5. In one to two sentences, explain why achieving your goal is important to you. What is in it for you?

6. What exact outcome do you plan to achieve?

7. Where will your outcome's area of impact be?

8. When will you achieve this outcome?

9. How will you go about achieving the outcome?

10. Why does this outcome support your application theme?

11. Write a draft sentence that incorporates the answers to question 6 - 10 in a single goal statement.

12. If your goal requires any sequential steps, write out each step and the deadline for that step to ensure that you meet your overall completion deadline.

13. What external support (funding, cooperation, permission, etc.) does your goal require?

14. For each support you listed in question 13, describe how you plan to secure it, or if it is impossible to secure, write an alternative final goal that will not require that support.

15. What obstacles do you face in your goal? Consider physical, technological, political, and personal obstacles.

16. For each obstacle in question 15, write how you will overcome or avoid it.

17. What specific aspect of your goal will you measure to determine when it is complete (or how close it is to being complete)?

18. If you had to change your end goal because of obstacles or reliance on outside support, rewrite your goal statement with the new final objective.

Why Your Goal Requires Study in Japan

19. How does your goal require additional, original research?

20. If you cannot identify a clear relationship between the need for research and your goal, rewrite your goal statement so that it requires research, knowledge, understanding, or technology that you do not yet have access to, but can acquire during your time in Japan.

21. Why does your research have to be conducted in Japan, or at a particular university in Japan?

22. List all the ways you can think of that your efforts to attain your post-graduation goal could strengthen the relationship between your home country and Japan.

23. List any supporting activities related to your goal that you could do to promote connections between your home country and Japan after graduation.

Considering Your Opposition's Needs

24. How can attaining your goal lead to you becoming a leader in your home country, so that you can be an effective cultural ambassador for Japan? Include the field where you plan to become a leader.

25. (Especially if you are applying for the Embassy recommendation) How does your goal serve your home country?

26. What value does your research plan offer to a potential adviser in Japan?

Your Superpowers

27. What do you do better than most people around you?

28. What do other people come to you for help with?

29. What are you so passionate about that you would do it all day, even if you weren't getting paid?

30. When you work in a group, what task do you usually take on?

31. Ask your friends or family what they think you are good at and write those down, too.

32. What are the common underlying abilities that support each of your superpowers?

Leveraging Your Past

33. What academic experiences do you have (top grades, study abroad, research assistantship, publications, presentations, etc.)? List each experience and at least one way that you can connect that experience to your goal for your MEXT scholarship or to one of your superpowers that will give you an advantage over other applicants.

34. List the languages other than Japanese or English where you have any proficiency and your level (academic, daily conversation, minimal).
34.a. For any academic-level proficiency, how can you use that to serve your research interest in Japan? Are there particular advantages that language offers?
34.b. For daily conversation or minimal proficiency, how can you use that ability to show your adaptability to new cultures and/or willingness to interact?

35. List any professional certifications you have related to your field of study and connect them to your specific research.

36. List any professional certifications you have that are *not* related to your field of study. Is there some way you can leverage them to show your dedication and follow-through ability, while also connecting them to your goal in Japan?

37. What experience do you have with Japanese culture or working with Japanese people? For each one, list the experience and one or two ways that having that experience makes you better prepared to adjust to life in Japan.

38. What, if any, disadvantages or obstacles might hold back your application? For each one, list a justification that connects to your goal.

Appendix A: GPA Conversion Charts

Converting your GPA to MEXT's strange 3.0 system can be the most challenging part of determining whether or not your are eligible - or competitive - for the scholarship.

The conversion conversion calculation depends on your country and/or university's grading system, so there is no one-size-fits-all solution, but in this appendix, I will explain the process and give as many examples as possible so that you can find the conversion that works for you.

Explanation of the Grading System

When you submit your academic transcript, or equivalent, one of MEXT's requirements is that it must include or be accompanied by an "Explanation of the Grading System". Many applicants get confused by this requirement.

A grading system is a chart or list showing all of the possible grades, marks, or scores you could have earned in any given class and what the various grades mean. The chart should explain which grades are considered to be excellent, good, average, poor, and failing. They do not necessarily need to use those labels, so long as there is a clear stratification. In this appendix, I share several examples so that you will know what to look for. Sometimes, this information is on the transcript, itself. In other cases it isn't, or there isn't enough detail. In those cases, you would need to submit additional documentation from your university.

Grading systems can be very different. Even if they use the same letters or numbers, the respective values can differ as we will see in the examples below. That is why you need to show exactly which system applies for your university. For example, in the US (and Japan) a "70" is a poor grade, barely passing. But in the UK, it could be a top grade.

Grade Buckets

I use the term "grade bucket" to mean a group of grades that all have the same converted value. For example, the grades "A+", "A", and "A-" might be considered one grade bucket. Or the a score range of "100 - 80" might be a single grade bucket.

When you convert your grades, you will need to determine how many buckets your system has and which grades correspond to each bucket. Typically, you should have 4 or 5 buckets. Multiple grades may fit into each of those buckets, as we will show in the examples below.

In some cases, you may encounter a system with only three buckets (e.g. distinction, pass, fail), but these are quite rare. I will explain that system below as well. For systems with more than 5 apparent buckets, like ECTS grades with 6, we will squeeze them into 5, using the charts that follow.

There are a few complications you may run into in assigning your grades to different buckets are subgrades or the average marks system.

For subgrades, such as +/- or combined grades like A/B, refer to the explanation of the grading system from your university. If your grading system does not explain the subgrades, you can *probably* ignore the "+" and "-", but if you want a more conservative estimate, treat "-" grades as the next lower bucket.

Note: Grades followed by a 0, such as A0, B0, etc., are not subgrades. Treat them as being the same as an A or B, respectively.

Average Marks

If your university uses the Average Marks System of adding total earned marks and dividing by the total available marks, while not giving specific grades for each class, you still need to convert based on the percentage of marks you earned in each individual class. You would use the same percentages as you do for the overall marks conversion. In that case, multiply each grade by the total number of marks available for the class, instead of credits.

Conversion for Reference, Only

I have included charts for specific countries and universities that I have direct experience with (transcripts or official explanations on university websites that I have checked and confirmed), but please note that these conversions are based only on my experience and how we did things. These are not guaranteed rules and may be up to interpretation.

Ultimately, the score that you convert is not going to be your official score. The university or embassy will not accept your math. They will convert it themselves, and use their results for processing your application. The point in doing the conversion yourself is just to make sure you are eligible in advance.

Grading Systems with Examples and Conversion Charts

In the rest of this appendix you will find examples of several different grading systems with conversion charts for each, as well as images of the grading system explanation taken from transcripts from various universities.

The images below come from scans of transcripts or websites that I have used or that past applicants have sent me. The quality may vary as most of these are scans of copies of transcripts that applicants have sent me over the years. If none of the grading systems below matches yours and you want me to add yours to the examples, please submit a scan or image of your grading system (I don't need to see your actual grades) via the form below:

https://mymext.com/submitgrades

Note: Since this form includes a file upload option, you must have a google account to use it.

Letter Grade Systems

Letter grade systems, typically A through E or F, are common in many countries, including the US, most of Europe (ECTS), many universities in East and Southeast Asia, and of course, Japan. However, there are several different ways of interpreting the relative value of these grades. Typically, Japanese universities and embassies will interpret the grades according to their own understanding, unless you have a grading scale to show them otherwise.

Letter grades can have pluses (e.g. A+), minuses (e.g. A-), zeroes (e.g. A0), or combined letters (e.g. A/B), which complicate the interpretation. I will include as many examples as possible below.

MEXT offers two official examples of how to convert letter grades to its 3.0 scale: A 4-bucket system and a 5-bucket system.

Letter Grades: 4 Letters (ABCF), Official

Grading System: ABCF (Official)				
Local Grade	A	B	C	F
MEXT Grade	3	2	1	0
Used in: Example from official MEXT guidelines, Taiwan				

This is the official example from MEXT, but I have only ever seen it used for graduate programs. For graduate programs, a "C" is typically considered the minimum passing grade and expectations are higher in general.

Here is an example of a grading system showing this scale, for **graduate** grades.

Systems : UG=Undergraduate : PG=Postgraduate
Grade remark: # = Exempt; W = Withdraw; TR = Transfer Credit.   Page 1
For Undergraduate: 60 is the passing grade
   80 or More = **A** (G.P.A.4); 70 to 79 = **B** (G.P.A.3); 60 to 69 = **C** (G.P.A.2); 50 to 59 = **D** (G.P.A.1); 49 & Below = **F** (G.P.A.0)
For Graduate: 70 is the passing grade
   85 or More = **A** (G.P.A.4); 75 to 84 = **B** (G.P.A.3); 70 to 74 = **C** (G.P.A.2); 69 & Below = **F** (G.P.A.0)

Of course, citizens of Taiwan are not eligible to apply for the MEXT scholarship, but international students who graduate from Taiwanese universities would be eligible.

Letter Grades: 5 Letters (ABCDF, etc.), Official

MEXT offers two official 5-bucket letter grade conversion scales, but I have never seen the first one used:

Grading System: Official: SABCF				
Local Grade	S	A	B	C	F
MEXT Grade	3	3	2	1	0
Used in: Example from official MEXT guidelines				

The one I do see more commonly is:

Grading System: Official: ABCDF				
Local Grade	A	B	C	D	F
MEXT Grade	3	3	2	1	0
Used in: Example from official MEXT guidelines, Taiwan				

The image above shows this example in the for **undergraduate** grades.

Most often, you will see this system with pluses and minuses, as in the example below.

Letter Grades: 5 Letters, with Plus/Minus

The rest of the letter grade conversion tables are *not official*. These are based on examples and methods that I have personally used, but in some places they may be up for interpretation.

Five letter systems with pluses and minuses are, by far, the most common system I see. There are several different variations on the system. Some universities may use only pluses and no minuses. Some may specify a non-plus/minus grade with a zero (such as "A0") to make it impossible to forge into a plus later. Some may use "E" for a failing grade and some may use "F".

I will list all of the most common variants in the table below, but keep in mind that not all of the grades listed in each bucket may apply to you, as you will be able to see from the example images below. That is not a problem.

There are a few important exceptions to this chart, regarding minuses, that we will cover below.

Grading System: ABCDF (with +/-)				
Local Grade	A+, A, A-	B+, B, B-	C+, C, C-	D+, D, D-	E or F
MEXT Grade	3	3	2	1	0
Used in: Brunei, Canada, Hong Kong, Korea, Macau, Malaysia, Singapore, Thailand, USA					

Examples:

Grade	Standard	Grade Point
A+ A A-	Excellent	4.0 4.0 3.7
B+ B B-	Good	3.3 3.0 2.7
C+ C C-	Satisfactory	2.3 2.0 1.7
D+ D	Pass	1.3 1.0
F	Fail	0.0
*P	Ungraded pass	Not included in GPA calculation
*DI	Distinction	

* The grades of Distinction and Ungraded pass only apply to some courses

In this example, the descriptions of each grade level makes it very easy to know which grades belong in which bucket. If you have a similar system that shows standards like the example above, use that as your guide to understand how to group your grades.

GRADE DESCRIPTION

A = 4	Points(Excellent)	D+ = 1.5	Points(Rather poor)	P =	In progress
B+ = 3.5	Points(Very good)	D = 1	Point (Poor)	S =	Satisfactory
B = 3	Points(Good)	F = 0	(Fail)	U =	Unsatisfactory
C+ = 2.5	Points(Fairly good)	AU =	Audit	W =	Withdrawal
C = 2	Points(Fair)	I =	Incomplete	X =	No report from teacher
				T =	Transfer of Credit

This example shows what a grading scale would look like with no minuses and no A+. This does not change how grades are sorted using the chart above.

```
2. Grading Scale : A+ : 4.5, A0 : 4.0, B+ : 3.5, B0 : 3.0, C+ : 2.5, C0 : 2.0, D+ : 1.5, D0 : 1.0, F : 0.0
```

Here's an example showing a university that uses zeroes to designate a neutral grade. In that case, an "A0" would be an "A" in the chart above.

Letter Grades: 5 Letters, with Plus/Minus - Variations

I mentioned above that there are some exceptions to the chart above. The most dangerous one is grading systems that specify that a minus grade should be considered to be grouped with the next lower letter grade. As you can imagine, this can have a significant effect on your overall GPA calculation.

Here's what the conversion chart would look like:

Grading System: ABCDF (drop -)				
Local Grade	A+, A	A-, B+, B	B-, C+, C	C-, D+, D	F
MEXT Grade	3	3	2	1	0
Used in: Morocco					

Here's an example of they grading system explanation that would result in the chart above:

A+ A	4 4.00	Excellent
A- B+ B	3.67 3.33 3	Good
B- C+ C	2.67 2.33 2	Fair
C- D+ * D*	1.67 1.33 1	Pass
F	0	Fail

It is also possible that only some minuses would be dropped, like the example below, where a C- is dropped to be a failing grade.

Here's what the conversion chart would look like:

Grading System: University of Malaya					
Local Grade	A+	A, A-	B+, B, B-	C+, C	C-, D+, D, F
MEXT Grade	3	3	2	1	0
Used in: Malaysia					

Here is an example of that grading system:

MARKAH / MARKS	GRED / GRADE	MATA GRED / GRADE POINT	MAKSUD / MEANING
90 - 100	A+	4.0	Amat Cemerlang /Excellent
80 - 89	A	4.0	Cemerlang / Distinction
75 - 79	A-	3.7	Cemerlang / Distinction
70 - 74	B+	3.3	Kepujian / Good
65 - 69	B	3.0	Kepujian / Good
60 - 64	B-	2.7	Kepujian / Good
55 - 59	C+	2.3	Lulus / Pass
50 - 54	C	2.0	Lulus / Pass
45 - 49	C-	1.7	Gagal / Fail
40 - 44	D+	1.3	Gagal / Fail
35 - 39	D	1.0	Gagal / Fail
00 - 34	F	0.0	Gagal / Fail

Like the first example I gave of a 5-letter system with pluses and minuses, in a system with clear quality descriptions next to each group of letter grades, so those would take precedence.

Finally, in some cases, instead of a + or -, the university may combine both letters, as in the case below:

Here's what the conversion chart would look like:

Grading System: ABCDE (with "AB")				
Local Grade	A	AB, B	BC, C	D	E
MEXT Grade	3	3	2	1	0
Used in: Indonesia				

Here is an example of that grading system:

Index score table

Index	Score	Total Score	Description
A	4.0	≥80	Excellent
AB	3.5	75-79.9	Good to Excellent
B	3.0	65-74.9	Good
BC	2.5	60-64.9	Fair to Good
C	2.0	55-59.9	Fair
D	1.0	50-54.5	Insufficient
E	0.0	<50	Failed
T	–	–	Incomplete

Because the descriptions include both keywords for the letter above and letter below, it isn't completely clear how to sort them, but the other columns give a clue. If you compare the "score" column to the GPA values associated with most of the other systems here, you will see that the "BC" is equal to 2.5. This is below the usual "B-" cutoff of 2.7, so I would include it with the "C" grades ("2" on the MEXT scale). Note that the AB grade doesn't matter because both "A" and "B" are "3" on the MEXT scale.

Letter Grades: 3 or 4 Letters, with Plus/Minus

While not as common as 5-letter grading systems, you may find some 4-letter grading systems with pluses and minuses, which would be evaluated as below:

Grading System: ABCF with Specified Pass Cut-Off			
Local Grade	A+, A, A-	B+, B, B-	C+, C, C-	F
MEXT Grade	3	2	1	0
Used in: New Zealand, Taiwan			

Here is an example of that grading system:

Letter Grading System	Definition	Grade Points	Conversion Scale
A+	All goals achieved beyond expectation	4.3	90 - 100
A	All goals achieved	4.0	85 - 89
A-	All goals achieved, but need some polish	3.7	80 - 84
B+	Some goals well achieved	3.3	77 - 79
B	Some goals adequately achieved	3.0	73 - 76
B- (passing grade for graduate students)	Some goals achieved with minor flaws	2.7	70 - 72
C+	Minimum goals achieved	2.3	67 - 69
C	Minimum goals achieved with minor flaws	2.0	63 - 66
C- (passing grade for undergraduate students)	Minimum goals achieved with major flaws	1.7	60 - 62
F	Minimum goals not achieved	0	59 AND BELOW
X	Not graded due to unexcused absences or other reasons	0	0
W	Withdrawal		
NG	No grade reported		
IP	In progress		
TR	Transfer credit		
EX	Exempted		

As you can see in this example, B- is the minimum passing grade for a graduate student. So, if you were converting graduate program grades, than a C+, C, and C- would be grouped in with the failing grades and calculated as zero points. (It would not be possible for a graduate level grade to convert to a "1" in this system.)

Letter Grades: ECTS

ECTS, the common standard in Europe, is a 6-bucket system and, in general grades earned under the ECTS system are "harsher" than those under the US or Japanese systems. For example, World Education Services (WES), an internationally recognized company that maintains conversion tables from almost all countries' systems to the US 4.0 system, converts an ECTS "C" to an American "B" for GPA purposes (3.0 out of 4.0 in the US, which is 3.0 out of 3.0 on the MEXT Scale).

If you are a European applying via the Embassy-Recommended MEXT Scholarship, you do not need to worry, since all other applicants will have been graded on the same system and the embassy should be familiar with it.

However, if you completed your degree at a European university but are applying for Embassy-Recommended MEXT Scholarship in another country, or if you are applying for University-Recommended MEXT Scholarship, the reviewers might not realize that ECTS grades are stricter than other countries' letter grades. In that case, it might be in your interest to include an official chart from your university that shows the equivalency between ECTS and US letter grades, for example. Ask your university's study abroad or admissions office if they have something like that you can reference! If your grading system also has quality descriptions, as in the first example below, that would work fine, too.

Here are two ways to interpret ECTS letter grades. The first is how I would do it, based on my experience working with hundreds of students from across Europe. The second, strict, model is how someone who did not understand ECTS might interpret your grades. If you want to be strict on yourself, for the sake of making sure that you meet the eligibility criteria, use the second scale. Remember, your conversion is not official, anyway, so you can not hurt yourself be being harsh.

ECTS Scale 1:

Grading System: ECTS				
Local Grade	A, B	C	D	E	Fx, F
MEXT Grade	3	3	2	1	0
Used in: Europe				

ECTS Scale 2 (Strict):

Grading System: ECTS (Strict)				
Local Grade	A	B	C	D, E	Fx, F
MEXT Grade	3	3	2	1	0
Used in: Europe				

Examples:

Level	ECTS Grade	Value
Excellent	A	1
Very good	B	1,5
Good	C	2
Satisfactory	D	2,5
Sufficient	E	3
Failed	F	4

The Grading Scale

Danish Grade	Definition	ECTS Grade
12	For an excellent performance displaying a high level of command of all aspects of the relevant material, with no or only a few minor weaknesses.	A
10	For a very good performance displaying a high level of command of most aspects of the relevant material, with only minor weaknesses.	B
7	For a good performance displaying good command of the relevant material but also some weaknesses.	C
4	For a fair performance displaying some command of the relevant material but also some major weaknesses.	D
02	For a performance meeting only the minimum requirements for acceptance.	E
00	For a performance which does not meet the minimum requirements for acceptance.	Fx
-3	For a performance which is unacceptable in all respects.	F

Both grading systems above clearly show that "E" is a passing grade, and "D" is "fair" or "satisfactory", which is the same definition given to a C grade in the examples further above, so "E" should be the only 1-point value and "D" should be 2. The real question is how to treat "C". In these examples, "C" is "Good", as opposed to its meaning of "Average" in the US system. Therefore, it should be considered to be equivalent to a US "B" (also good) and scored at 3 points on the MEXT scale.

Percentage Scales

Like letter grades, the meaning of percentages can vary significantly from country to country. There seem to be two major philosophical outlooks on what the percentage should mean.

In countries like the US and Japan, where you tend to see high grades, the score seems to indicate what percentage of the mastery or performance *expected of a student in the course* you have achieved. In this system, students should be aiming for 100%.

In Europe, the UK, and countries with marks systems, the score seems to indicate instead what percentage of *mastery of the subject* you have achieved. In that case, even the professor might not earn 100% and for a student, earning 70% would be outstanding.

Think about your own system and the normative scores there as you read through the systems and charts below.

Percentage Grades: 4 Buckets, Official

Grading System: Official: Percentage			
Local Grade	100 - 80	79 - 70	69 - 60	59 - 0
MEXT Grade	3	2	1	0
Used in: Example from official MEXT guidelines, Taiwan			

Example:

Remarks : 100 is the full mark

80 - 100=A=4   50 - 59=D=1

70 - 79=B=3   49 and below=E=0

60 - 69=C=2   For the graduate students.the passing grade is 70.

W : withdraw   For the undergraduate students.the passing grade is 60.

This is one of MEXT's official guidelines for converting percentages. Like the 4-Letter system we discussed at the top, you would primarily see this system used for graduate grades, as in the example below (Note that for undergraduate grades, there are 5 buckets).

Percentage Grades: 5 Buckets, Official

MEXT's official standard for converting 5 percentage score buckets is based on how percentages are assigned in Japan, where 100% is achievable for students.

Grading System: Official: Percentage					
Local Grade	100 - 90	89 - 80	79 - 70	69 - 60	59 - 0
MEXT Grade	3	3	2	1	0
Used in: Example from official MEXT guidelines, USA, Mongolia, China					

The example image I used for the 4-bucket system above would be a 5-range scale for undergraduates. Here is another example of what that score system might look like.

scores	100-90	89-80	79-70	69-60	≤ 59
grades	Excellent	Good	Average	Pass	Fail

Percentage Grades: 5 Buckets, Variations

Some universities have a more "lenient" percentage scale. Although, any apparent leniency in the system is usually a reflection of how much more difficult it is to earn the corresponding grades.

Grading System: Canada Percentage					
Local Grade	100 - 80	79 - 70	69 - 60	59 - 50	49 - 0
MEXT Grade	3	3	2	1	0
Used in: Canada					

Example:

Percentage	Letter Grade	Grade Point Value	Grade Meanings
90-100	A+	4.0	Excellent
85-89	A	4.0	Excellent
80-84	A-	3.7	Excellent
77-79	B+	3.3	Good
73-76	B	3.0	Good
70-72	B-	2.7	Good
67-69	C+	2.3	Adequate
63-66	C	2.0	Adequate
60-62	C-	1.7	Adequate
57-59	D+	1.3	Marginal
53-56	D	1.0	Marginal
50-52	D-	0.7	Marginal
0-49	F	0.0	Inadequate

With percentages, letters, GPA, and quality descriptions, this is a simple system to interpret.

In some universities, you will find grading systems with percentage buckets, but different cutoffs, as below. In this case, use the cutoff specified in your university's grading system!

Here is one example from the Philippines:

Grading System: Philippines Percentage				
Local Grade	100 - 91.5	91.25 - 86	85.75 - 80.5	80.25 - 75	74.75 - 0
MEXT Grade	3	3	2	1	0
Used in: Philippines				

In the example below, I'm not completely sure if it is possible to earn grades that fall between the cutoffs for the percentages, but to be as safe as possible, I treated the percentage shown for each descriptor to be the bottom of the bucket for that level.

The equivalent in percentage, letter grade and grade points of the UP grade are as follows:

UP GRADE		Percentage	Letter Grade	Grade Points
1.0	EXCELLENT	97-100	A	4.0
1.25		94.25	A-	3.625
1.5	VERY GOOD	91.5	B+	3.25
1.75		88.75	B	2.875
2.00	GOOD	86	B-	2.5
2.25		83.25	C+	2.125
2.50	SATISFACTORY	80.5	C	1.75
2.75		77.75	C-	1.375
3.0	PASS	75	D	1
4.0	CONDITIONAL			
5.0	FAIL	Fail	F	0
INC.	INCOMPLETE			

Descriptive Grades

I have found descriptive grades to be common in Commonwealth countries. In this system, the grades are stratified by a description of their quality, not immediately obvious letter or number scales. Probably the best well-known is the Honours system used in the UK, though others exist.

Descriptive Grades: 4 Buckets, Official

The system below will look familiar to you if you have completed the MEXT scholarship application form, particularly the part where you have to rate your language ability.

Grading System: Official: Description			
Local Grade	優 (Excellent)	良 (Good)	可 (pass)	不可 (Fail)
MEXT Grade	3	2	1	0
Used in: Example from official MEXT guidelines			

While this is an official conversion scale, I have never seen a university that uses it.

MEXT does not offer an official conversion scale for 5-bucket descriptive grades. However, in practice, every descriptive system I have seen had 5 buckets. Those systems would be converted just like any other 5-bucket system.

Descriptive Grades: 5-Bucket Honours

I believe all Honours grades should be converted on a 5-bucket scale. The scale below, from a UK university, shows how this could be done.

Grading System: Honours System (with third)					
Local Grade	First Class	Upper Second	Lower Second	Third	Fail
MEXT Grade	3	3	2	1	0
Used in: UK					

Example:

Honours	General	CAS	CGS	US
First Class	Outstanding	20	A1, A2	A+
		19	A3	A
		18	A4, A5	A
Upper second	Very Good	17	B1	A-
		16	B2	B+
		15	B3	B+
Lower second	Good	14	C1	B
		13	C2	B
		12	C3	B-
Third	Pass	11	D1	C+
		10	D2	C
		9	D3	C-
Fail	Marginal Fail	8	E1	D
		7	E2	D
		6	E3	D
	Clear Fail	0-5	F1, F2, F3 G1, G2, G3	F

In Honours systems, you usually do not get an "Honours" mark for each individual course, so when converting your grades, convert each course based on how your score in that individual course would correspond to the honours ranking if that was your overall grade for your degree. For example, in the scale above, from the University of Aberdeen, students grades in each course are indicated using the marks shown in the CGS column. So, if you received a B3 in a particular course, that corresponds to an Upper Second, and so it would be a "3" on the MEXT Scale.

Another way to think of this system is that we are using the Honours titles (First Class, Upper Second, etc.) in place of the quality description (Outstanding, Good, etc.) as a frame of reference. Yes, the scale above also includes quality descriptions, but not all will!

The trouble with Honours systems is that sometimes they do not include a "Third Class" bucket. In that case, reviewers who are not familiar with the system may consider a "Lower Second" to be the minimum passing grade (i.e. "1" on the MEXT Scale), making "Upper Second" a "2". It would be almost impossible to achieve the minimum 2.3 grade in that situation.

Descriptive Grades: Distinction

Another descriptive grading system is the Distinction system used by some universities in Australia and New Zealand. The first time I reviewed a transcript on this system, I was shocked to see that the student had earned all "C" and "D" grades. At first glance, I thought there was no way this student could be eligible, until I saw what those letters meant!

Grading System: Distinction Marking					
Local Grade	HD (High Distinction) 100 - 80	D (Distinction) 79 - 70	C (Credit) 69 - 60	P (Pass) 59 - 50	N (Fail) 49 - 0
MEXT Grade	3	3	2	1	0
Used in: Australia					

Example:

HD	High distinction	80% plus
D	Distinction	70%-79%
C	Credit	60%-69%
P	Pass	50%-59%
UP	Ungraded pass	
EP	External institution pass	
PC	Pass conceded	
N	Fail	
XN	Failure, not assessed	
NP	Pass following supplementary examination (withdrawn from use in 1994)	
NN	Failure following supplementary examination (withdrawn from use in 1994)	
WL	Withdrawn without academic penalty	
WN	Withdrawn fail	
WR	Withdrawn, debt remission	
WRN	Withdrawn, debt remission, academic penalty	

Descriptive Grades: 3 Buckets

One applicant sent me a copy of a 3-bucket descriptive grading system. These grades were from an open university, where faculty would not have much time to focus on individual students. Most students simply get a "satisfactory", or passing, grade in each course if they do the work. Unfortunately, since that is the lowest possible passing grade, it could get converted to a 1 on the MEXT scale. Personally, I would consider it to be a "2", since "Satisfactory" as a quality description is consistent with the description of grades in other systems that count as "2"s. But even as a "2", this would make it essentially impossible to meet the MEXT eligibility requirements.

If your only degree program is in an open university or other university that similarly does not give much time or care to grading students, you will face significant difficulty in the application. If you are taking an open university degree program *alongside* a regular university's degree program, then it may serve your interests to withdraw from or suspend your open university courses during the application period, and report that you only intend to complete your regular university degree, so that only the regular university degree will count for the GPA calculation.

Grading System: 3-Bucket Descriptive			
Local Grade	Honor	Satisfactory	Unsatisfactory
MEXT Grade	3	2	0
Used in: Open universities			

Example:

Educational Evaluation

Grading System

H or H*	=	Honor	76 - 100%	(4.0)
S or S*	=	Satisfactory	60 - 75%	(2.3)
U or U*	=	Unsatisfactory	0 - 59%	(0.0)
*	=	re - examination		

Numerical Grading Scales and GPA

While MEXT's 3.0 GPA system is not actually used anywhere in the world that I am aware of, I have seen a number of other GPA systems or numerical grading scales.

The most common GPA scale is the 4.0 scale. I have also seen 4.3, common in Korea, 4.5 in some universities in Canada, 5.0 in Singapore and many others. However, in each of the examples above, the universities in question also had letter grades or percentage grades listed, so it was easier to convert the grades using that information. If your university has multiple grading scales including a numerical grading system and another, such as letters or percentages, I recommend that you use the letter of percentage grades to perform your conversion. If only the numbers are shown for your grades in each course, first convert those to the corresponding letter or percentage, then convert to MEXT's system. That is the approach your reviewers are likely to take, too. Most of the examples below include multiple systems.

In this section, I will focus on universities that use numbers as their grades, to show the variety of systems. Unless you find an exact match for your grading system below, you should not assume that numbers mean the same thing in your country, but I hope this section will give you an idea of what to look for when trying to figure out how to convert number systems.

Numerical: 4-Point Inverted Scale

While a 4.0 GPA system with 4 being the best score is relatively common around the world, there are some systems where 1 is the best score, as shown below.

This particular university also uses ECTS scores, but there may be some universities that only show one or the other.

Grading System: 1 (best) - 4 (worst) Scale				
Local Grade	1	1,5 - 2	2,5	3	4
MEXT Grade	3	3	2	1	0
Used in: Czech Republic (also uses ECTS)				

Example:

Level	ECTS Grade	Value
Excellent	A	1
Very good	B	1,5
Good	C	2
Satisfactory	D	2,5
Sufficient	E	3
Failed	F	4

Numerical: 5-Point Scale

The Finnish example below uses a 5-point scale but has no numerical grade designated for failure, so all grades shown in numbers will have at least some value.

Grading System: 5-Point Scale					
Local Grade	5	4 - 3	2	1	(none)
MEXT Grade	3	3	2	1	0
Used in: Finland					

Example:

Grading Scale:
5 =excellent
4 =very good
3 = good
2 = satisfactory
1 = sufficient
hyv. = passed, no grading
kiit. = passed with distinction

Numerical: 5-Point Inverted Scale

We used this scale earlier to highlight a different approach to percentages, but it also contains a number system. As with the percentage, The quality descriptor is the key factor for the conversion. Unlike the system above, in this case, "1" is the highest grade and "5" is a fail.

Grading System: Philippines 5-point system					
Local Grade	1.0 - 1.5	1.75 - 2.0	2.25 - 2.5	2.75 - 3.0	4.0 - 5.0
MEXT Grade	3	3	2	1	0
Used in: Philippines					

Example:

The equivalent in percentage, letter grade and grade points of the UP grade are as follows:

UP GRADE		Percentage	Letter Grade	Grade Points
1.0	EXCELLENT	97-100	A	4.0
1.25		94.25	A-	3.625
1.5	VERY GOOD	91.5	B+	3.25
1.75		88.75	B	2.875
2.00	GOOD	86	B-	2.5
2.25		83.25	C+	2.125
2.50	SATISFACTORY	80.5	C	1.75
2.75		77.75	C-	1.375
3.0	PASS	75	D	1
4.0	CONDITIONAL			
5.0	FAIL	Fail	F	0
INC.	INCOMPLETE			

Numerical: Danish "7"-Point Scale

I have heard this scale called a seven-point scale by my colleagues in Denmark, despite the fact that the grades range from a high of 12 to a low of -3, since there are only 7 discrete grades that can be earned.

If you are in Denmark, then the range of grades may matter for calculating averages, but remember that for MEXT, we never take the average. We always convert grade-by-grade.

Grading System: Danish 7-point Scale					
Local Grade	12 - 10	7	4	02	00 - -3
MEXT Grade	3	3	2	1	0
Used in: Denmark (Also uses ECTS)					

Example:

The Grading Scale

Danish Grade	Definition	ECTS Grade
12	For an excellent performance displaying a high level of command of all aspects of the relevant material, with no or only a few minor weaknesses.	A
10	For a very good performance displaying a high level of command of most aspects of the relevant material, with only minor weaknesses.	B
7	For a good performance displaying good command of the relevant material but also some weaknesses.	C
4	For a fair performance displaying some command of the relevant material but also some major weaknesses.	D
02	For a performance meeting only the minimum requirements for acceptance.	E
00	For a performance which does not meet the minimum requirements for acceptance.	Fx
-3	For a performance which is unacceptable in all respects.	F

Numerical/GPA: Vietnamese 10-Point GPA

Vietnamese universities grade on a 10-point GPA scale, though some also use letter grades. Although the system is referred to as a GPA scale, students are actually assigned a grade on the 10-point scale for each class. It is those individual course grades, not the overall average, that must be converted. Here is one example:

Grading System: 10.0 GPA Scale				
Local Grade	10.0 - 8.5	8.4 - 7.0	6.9 - 5.5	5.4 - 4.0	3.9 - 0
MEXT Grade	3	3	2	1	0
Used in: Vietnam					

Example:

Notes:
(1) The following are commonly used to converse from ten-point grade to letter grade: A+: 9.0 - 10.0; A: 8.5 - 8.9; B+: 8.0 - 8.4; B: 7.0 - 7.9; C+: 6.5 - 6.9; C: 5.5 - 6.4; D+: 5.0 - 5.4; D: 4.0 - 4.9; F: Below 4.0;
(2) From letter grate to four-point grade: A+ = 4.0; A = 3.7; B+ = 3.5; B = 3.0; C+ = 2.5; C = 2.0; D+ = 1.5; D = 1.0; F = 0.0.
(3) Graduation Ranking: 3.60 - 4.00: High Distinction ; 3.20 - 3.59: Distinction; 2.50 - 3.19: Credit; 2.00 - 2.49: Pass.
(4) (*), (**), (***) is hight credits
(5) The codes marked with letter E in their endings are for courses delivered in English

The system above offers conversions to multiple other scales, but the letter grades are the most relevant for our conversion.

Numerical: 12-Point Scale

The university in the example below also shows the letter grade conversion, but course grades on the actual transcript may be shown by numerical value, only.

Grading System: Canadian 12-point Scale				
Local Grade	12 - 10	9 - 7	6 - 4	3 - 1	0
MEXT Grade	3	3	2	1	0
Used in: Canada					

Note that the conversion above applies only to undergraduate grades from the example below. For graduate grades, a 7 is considered the minimum passing grade, so 12 - 10 would be a 3, and 9 - 7 would be a 2. Everything else would be a zero.

Undergraduate and Qualifying Students

A+	12	B+	9	C+	6	D+	3
A	11	B	8	C	5	D	2
A-	10	B-	7	C-	4	D-	1
						F	0

Faculty of Graduate & Postdoctoral Studies
Master's and Doctoral Students

A+	12	B+	9	F	0
A	11	B	8		
A-	10	B-	7		

Numerical: French 20-Point Scale

Grading in France is particularly severe.

My colleagues there tell me that it is because everyone who passes that high school leaving exam has the right to go to higher education in public universities. There is no competition to get in to universities. So, the only way they can reduce their student numbers and get rid of the students who have no particular interest or aptitude is by failing them out. It is an achievement just to pass and remain enrolled, and the grading scale below reflects that.

Grading System: French 20-point Scale				
Local Grade	20 - 16	15 - 12	11	10 - 9	8 - 0
MEXT Grade	3	3	2	1	0
Used in: France				

Example:

French System	Letter Grade (US)	ECTS Grade	ECTS Grade
19-20	A+		Perfection
17-18	A	A	Exceptional
16	A-		Excellent
15	B+		Very good
14	B	B	Good
12-13	B-	C	Solid, Above expectations
11	C+	D	Acceptable
10	C		Passing grade – Very average, barely satisfactory
9	C-	E	Unsatisfactory
8	D+	FX	Lacks basic knowledge
6-7	D		Poor
5	D-		Very poor
3-4	F+	F	Little, if any knowledge
0-2	F		No knowledge

While this system offers a conversion to US grades, too, I have used the ECTS grades as a guide for the conversion, since that is the dominant system for grade conversion within Europe.

Numerical: Italian 30-Point Scale

The Italian system also has a wide range of grades, but most of the passing grades are concentrated at the top. I have seen many cases where universities did not provide any conversion guidance with their own transcripts, but here is a guide that should work. It provides handy conversions to a wide variety of systems.

Grading System: Italian 30-point Scale				
Local Grade	30 lode - 29	28 - 25	24 - 21	20 - 18	17 - 0
MEXT Grade	3	3	2	1	0
Used in: Italy				

Example:

Italian (exams and coursework)	American	British	French and Belgian	Chinese	Qualitative description
29-30 lode	A	First class (70 or more)	17-20	优秀	Excellent (distinction)
25-28	B	Upper second class (60-69)	14-16	良好	Very good
21-24	C	Lower second class (50-59	12-13	中等	Good
18-20	D	Third class (40-49)	10-11	及格	Adequate
17 or less	F	Fail (39 or less)	0-9		Not adequate

Final thoughts

Remember, the tables above correspond to the images. In most cases, the examples I have provided are consistent within the countries listed, to the best of my knowledge, but if the explanation of the grading system that your university provides is different from what the images above show, then always prioritize the documentation from your university.

Have a system I haven't covered above?

I will add new grading systems that I find after publication to an article on my website at the link below:

https://mymext.com/grades

If your grading system isn't covered by any of the examples above, submit a scan of the grading system to me via the form below and I will add it to the article above.

https://mymext.com/submitgrades

Note: Since this form includes a file upload option, you must have a google account to use it.

Sample Calculations

Why Can't You Just Convert Your Final Average?

It would be easier, right? But it wouldn't be accurate and you would be wasting your time.

If you convert your overall average rather than converting individual courses and taking the average of those scores, you could end up with a number that is wildly inaccurate.

To demonstrate, let's look at two hypothetical students. Both students took 10 total courses and come from a 5-bucket system based on percentage grades, as follows:

Local Grade	100 - 90	89 - 80	79 - 70	69 - 60	59 - 0
MEXT Grade	3	3	2	1	0

OK, here are our students' grades:

	Student 1	Student 2
	Local Grade	Local Grade
Course 1	100	80
Course 2	59	60
Course 3	79	80
Course 4	100	80
Course 5	79	80
Course 6	79	80
Course 7	79	80
Course 8	79	80
Course 9	79	80
Course 10	79	80
Average (Local Grades)	81.2	78.1

Apparently, Student 1 did better than Student 2. Student 1's final average would convert to a perfect 3 on the MEXT Scale, if we convert just the average based on the chart above, while Student 2 would convert to a 2, and would not be eligible to apply for the scholarship.

Now, let's look at what happens if we convert the grades correctly, one-by-one, with the same two students.

	Student 1		Student 2	
	Local Grade	MEXT Converted Grade	Local Grade	MEXT Converted Grade
Course 1	100	3	80	3
Course 2	59	0	60	1
Course 3	79	2	80	3
Course 4	100	3	80	3
Course 5	79	2	80	3
Course 6	79	2	80	3
Course 7	79	2	80	3
Course 8	79	2	80	3
Course 9	79	2	80	3
Course 10	79	2	80	3
Average (MEXT Converted)		2.0		2.8

Now, Student 2 has the higher grade, 2.8 overall, which is both eligible and competitive. Student 1, on the other hand, isn't even eligible to apply.

If you look again at the grades above, you'll note that the difference between the students is that Student 1 earned the highest possible grades in each bucket, while student 2 earned the lowest grades in each bucket. Being on the high end, helped student 1 to have a higher overall average, but when you convert to the MEXT scale, there is no difference between a 100 in this example and an 80. So all that extra credit might have paid off anywhere else, but not for MEXT.

Now, of course I'm not suggesting that you should settle for the lowest grade in each grade bucket and not try harder, I'm just trying to point out why you have to be careful in converting your grade.

Appendix B: Definitions

MEXT:

The Japanese Ministry of Education, Culture, Sports, Science and Technology. If you put all of those letters together, you get MECSST, which is pronounced "MEXT".

You may also see the ministry called *Monbukagakusho* or *Monbusho*. The first is the official Japanese name and the second is the old Japanese name that still persists, especially among former scholarship winners. All mean the same thing.

JASSO:

The Japan Student Services Organization. JASSO is an quasi-governmental "Independent Administrative Institution" that supports MEXT's efforts. They are charged with providing information about education in Japan in English and Japanese and also administer payment of government scholarships, including the MEXT Scholarship, on behalf of MEXT.

Research Student (*kenkyūsei*):

When MEXT refers to the scholarship for "research students", they mean *kenkyūsei*. The better translation is "graduate student" and this term refers to all graduate-level students, whether enrolled in a degree-seeking program, or not.

In Japanese, each individual graduate school within a university is called a *kenkyūka*, or research division. *Kenkyū* literally means research, but this term is translated as "graduate school" in almost all situations. For some reason *kenkyūsei*, which is derived from "student enrolled in a *kenkyūka*" is translated as "research student".

Translated terms in Japan are frustratingly inconsistent like that.

Research Student (*hiseikisei*):

Universities use the term "research student" or "non-degree student" interchangeably to refer to a student who is affiliated with a graduate school, but is not enrolled in a degree program. As you can see, the word in Japanese is completely different, despite being translated into English with the same term as *kenkyūsei*. *Hiseikisei* literally means non-regular student (and you will also see it written that way) and can refer to pre-graduate students who have not yet been admitted to the degree program or temporary graduate-level students who have no intention of seeking a degree but just want to take courses and conduct research there.

Many MEXT scholarship winners, especially those who are selected through the Embassy-Recommended MEXT Scholarship, start their studies in Japan as *hiseikisei* research students.

Degree-Seeking Student:

A degree-seeking student is a student who has passed the entrance exam and been matriculated into the degree program, as opposed to a *hiseikisei*. You can be a degree-seeking student at any level (undergraduate, master's, or doctoral). Once you are a degree-seeking student, you are "on the clock" to complete your degree within the designated standard number of years of enrollment: four for undergraduates, two for master's degrees, and three for most doctoral degrees.

MEXT scholars who cannot complete their degrees within the designated standard years will lose the scholarship as soon as it becomes clear that they are unable to complete on time.

Master's Degree:

For this book, I will use the term master's degree to encompass all master's level degrees, whether academic or not.

In Japan, degrees like Master of Arts or Master of Science are considered to be academic degrees. There are also master's-level professional degrees (see below) that fall under this category, such as MBAs and professional master's in teaching, etc.

Doctoral Degree:

For this book, I will use the term doctoral degree to encompass all doctorate level degrees, whether academic or not.

5-year Doctoral Degree (Also called "integrated" or "combined" doctoral degree):

Some programs in Japan offer a 5-year doctoral degree program with no master's degree awarded in the interim. For the sake of the MEXT scholarship, you would still be considered a master's level student for the first two years, even though you would not earn a degree after that point, and would have to apply for a scholarship extension to cover your participation in the final three years, which would be considered a doctoral degree, from MEXT's point of view.

If you have an appropriate master's degree already, it may be possible to enter a 5-year doctoral degree from the third year of studies.

Professional Degree:

Professional degrees are degrees that are required for a specific job qualification, rather than "pure" academic degrees. Examples include MBA, MD, MDDS, DVS, JD, DBA, etc. There is no prejudice against professional degrees within the evaluation system, but like anything else, you would have to justify why it is the most appropriate degree for your goal.

Embassy-Recommended MEXT Scholarship:

The process of applying for the MEXT scholarship by submitting your application to the Japanese embassy or consulate in your home country. In this process, you will still need to contact universities later for Letters of Acceptance.

For more on the Embassy-Recommended MEXT Scholarship process, please see Chapter 1: Understanding the MEXT Scholarship.

University-Recommended MEXT Scholarship:

The process of applying for the MEXT scholarship by submitting your application to the university in Japan that you wish to attend. In this process, you do not need to go through the Japanese embassy, except for your visa paperwork after selection.

For more on the University-Recommended MEXT Scholarship process, please see Chapter 1: Understanding the MEXT Scholarship.

Priority Graduate Program:

This is a subset of the University-Recommended MEXT Scholarship. There are some university programs that are pre-approved by MEXT to be able to nominate a specific number of students each year for the scholarship with the guarantee that all will receive it, if eligible. Typically, these programs have very narrow eligibility requirements, for example, they may be limited to students with a particular nationality, in a specific degree program and level, and studying in a specific language. While the list of PGP programs is usually available, the eligibility criteria for each one is often not revealed. If you meet the eligibility criteria for one of these programs, then your competition level is much lower and your chances of winning the scholarship skyrocket, but it is almost impossible to know in advance.

Primary Screening:

The initial round of the application screening conducted at the embassy/consulate or university. This is the competitive round and determines who will be recommended to MEXT for the scholarship. If you pass the primary screening and are recommended to MEXT, you are practically guaranteed to receive the scholarship, so that is what this series of books will focus on.

Secondary Screening:

MEXT's screening of recommended candidates. Although this screening takes longer than the Primary Screening, it is not competitive. In general, MEXT is just double-checking the embassy or university's work to make sure you are eligible. The only time that I have heard of applicants being rejected during the Secondary Screening was in 2019, when budget cuts forced MEXT to reduce the number of scholarship slots after the application process had started. But that was a highly unusual situation (the government had just decided to make university education free for low-income Japanese families and needed to shift budget resources suddenly) and should not happen again.

University Placement:

In the Embassy-Recommended MEXT Scholarship, after the Secondary Screening, MEXT contacts the universities from your Placement Preference Form to ask them to formally accept you. If you have at least one Letter of Provisional Acceptance, this step should not be a problem, but if you have no Letters of Provisional Acceptance, then there is a possibility that you could lose the scholarship at this stage if no university accepts you.

Placement Preference Form:

One of the application documents that exists only in the Embassy-Recommended MEXT Scholarship application process. This is the form where you list your top three universities where you would like to enroll as well as your desired academic advisor at each one. I will cover the process of searching for universities and professors in more detail in Book 3 of this series: *How to Find your best Degree Program and Advisor for the MEXT Scholarship*

https://mymext.com/getmms3

Field of Study and Research Program Plan:

The most important application document under your control. This is where you explain what you want to research in Japan and why. It is so important that Book 2 of this series, *How to Write a Scholarship-Winning Field of Study and Research Program Plan*, is dedicated entirely to that one form.

https://mymext.com/getmms2

Certificate of Graduation:

This does *not* necessarily mean your diploma! A Certificate of Graduation is any official document from your university stating that you have met all of the requirements and completed your degree program, along with the date.

Certificate of Expected Graduation:

This is an official letter from your university stating when you are expected to complete your degree and graduate. It does not need to guarantee that you *will* graduate on that date (no university would guarantee that, because you still have to pass your classes). It is the university's guarantee that *it is possible* for you to meet all of your requirements and graduate on that date. In other words, they are only saying that it is not impossible for you to graduate on the given date.

If you have not yet graduated by the time you submit your application, then you need to provide this document in place of a Certificate of Graduation.

Certificate of Grades:

This can also be called an academic transcript, certificate of marks, record of performance, etc. It is the document that shows your academic performance in each class you have taken at your current university.

Explanation of Grading System:

This is a scale that shows what the various grades "mean" and their relative value. See Appendix A for examples of different kinds of grading systems.

Graduation Thesis:

This is the culminating paper or project for your degree. You will be asked to submit an abstract of your thesis for the screening process. Especially at the undergraduate level, not all degree programs have a final thesis. That is fine. If you do not have a thesis or final project, check with the Embassy or University for guidance. You may be asked to submit an abstract of a term paper related to your research or told that you do not need to submit anything.

Since the requirement is to submit an abstract, not the whole thesis, you can submit the abstract even if you have not written the final thesis yet.

Visa:

Japan uses the word "visa" differently from every other country I am aware of. In Japan, a visa is only permission to enter the country. Once you arrive in Japan and pass through immigration, you have used up your visa and no longer have one (except in the case of multiple-entry visas). Instead, you will have a Residence Status, which is your permission to stay in the country.

MEXT scholarship winners have a special student visa application process that bypasses the usual requirement to obtain a Certificate of Eligibility. You will receive more information about the process and specific instructions after selection, but you will only be able to obtain your student visa at the Japanese embassy or consulate in your home country that serves your place of residence.

Residence Status:

Once you pass through immigration in Japan, your visa becomes invalid and you receive a residence status, instead. Your residence status is your legal permission to live in Japan to pursue the activities listed in that status. MEXT scholarship winners will have a Student Residence Status.

It is possible to change your residence status while living in Japan. For example, after graduating, you could apply to change your status to a working status. However, you cannot change your residence status during your MEXT scholarship award period or you will lose the scholarship.

Appendix C: Priority Countries

Priority countries are important to consider if you are applying for the University-Recommended MEXT Scholarship. As of the 2023/2024 application cycle, only applicants from Priority Countries, shown in the table below, are eligible to be selected for the General Category of the University-Recommended MEXT Scholarship. Students who are not from Priority Countries may apply for PGP programs, but even in that case, at least 75% of the nominees from any particular PGP program must be from Priority Countries. This is calculated on a program-by-program basis, even if a particular university has more than one PGP program. So, if the program has 4-7 slots, they can nominate only *one* student from a non-Priority Country.

For the Embassy-Recommended MEXT Scholarship, this restriction does not apply, but it is likely that Priority Countries will have a larger number of scholarship places available.

List of Priority Countries

This is the most recent list of Priority Countries as of the time of publication, based on the 2023/2024 University-Recommended MEXT Scholarship cycle. I will explain where to find the most recent table below.

Africa

- Algeria

- Angola

- Benin

- Botswana

- Burkina Faso

- Burundi

- Cabo Verde

- Cameroon

- Central African Republic

- Chad

- Comoros

- Cote D'Ivoire

- Democratic Republic of the Congo

- Djibouti

- Egypt

- Equatorial Guinea

- Eritrea

- Ethiopia

- Gabon

- Gambia

- Ghana

- Guinea

- Guinea-Bissau

- Kenya

- Lesotho

- Liberia

- Libya

- Madagascar

- Malawi

- Mali

- Mauritania

- Mauritius

- Morocco

- Mozambique

- Namibia

- Niger

- Nigeria

- Republic of the Congo

- Rwanda

- Sao Tome and Principe

- Senegal

- Seychelles

- Sierra Leone

- Somalia

- South Africa

- South Sudan

- Sudan

- Swaziland/eSwatini

- Tanzania

- Togo

- Tunisia

- Uganda

- Zambia

- Zimbabwe

Americas

- Argentina

- Bolivia

- Brazil

- Canada

- Chile

- Columbia

- Ecuador

- Guyana

- Paraguay

- Peru

- Suriname

- Uruguay

- USA

- Venezuela

Asia

- Bangladesh

- Bhutan

- Brunei

- Cambodia

- India

- Indonesia

- Laos

- Malaysia

- Maldives

- Mongolia

- Myanmar

- Nepal

- Pakistan

- The Philippines

- Singapore

- Sri Lanka

- Thailand

- Vietnam

Europe

- Albania

- Andorra

- Armenia

- Austria

- Azerbaijan

- Belgium

- Bosnia and Herzegovina

- Bulgaria

- Croatia

- Cyprus

- Czech Republic

- Denmark

- Estonia

- Italy

- Finland

- France

- Georgia

- Germany

- Greece

- Hungary

- Iceland

- Ireland

- Kazakhstan

- Kosovo

- Kyrgyzstan

- Latvia

- Liechtenstein

- Lithuania

- Luxembourg

- Malta

- Moldova

- Monaco

- Montenegro

- The Netherlands

- North Macedonia

- Norway

- Poland

- Portugal

- Romania

- San Marino

- Serbia

- Slovakia

- Slovenia

- Spain

- Sweden

- Switzerland

- Tajikistan

- Turkmenistan

- Ukraine

- United Kingdom

- Uzbekistan

- Vatican City

Middle East

- Afghanistan

- Bahrain

- Iran

- Iraq

- Israel

- Jordan

- Kuwait

- Lebanon

- Oman

- Palestine

- Qatar

- Saudi Arabia

- Syria

- Türkiye

- UAE

- Yemen

Oceania and Pacific Islands

- Australia

- Cook Islands

- Fiji

- Kiribati

- Marshall Islands

- Micronesia

- Nauru

- New Zealand

- Niue

- Palau

- Papua New Guinea

- Samoa

- Solomon Islands

- Tonga

- Tuvalu

- Vanuatu

Who's Not on the List

The list above is so long, it might be more useful to consider the countries that aren't listed. In general, they fall into 4 categories:

- Countries Japan does not recognize (e.g. North Korea, Taiwan)

- China (including Hong Kong and Macau) and South

Korea (Note: These two countries alone make up over 46% of international students in Japan.)

- Central America and the Carribbean

- Russia and Belarus (Previously on the list, but removed after the invasion of Ukraine.)

Timor-Leste is also not on the list, but it didn't fit in any of the categories above.

List Updates

This list has changed several times since I published the first edition of this book, so if you're reading in 2024 or later, it may have changed again.

I update the list of priority countries each fall on my website when I update the articles about the University-Recommended MEXT Scholarship. You can find that information at the link below:

https://mymext.com/priority

The list is also available (in Japanese only) on the "Data" tab of the excel "List of Nominees" form that universities have to submit to MEXT. You can find that document on MEXT's website in the instructions for the University-Recommended MEXT Scholarship each year.

https://mymext.com/mextofficial

Appendix D: References and Resources

My MEXT Scholarship Resources

Bonus Document Pack including the GPA Calculation Tool

https://mymext.com/bonusmms1

Mastering the MEXT Scholarship: The Complete Series

https://mymext.com/mmsseries

My MEXT Scholarship Website
(Formerly TranSenzJapan.com)

My website with all of my articles about the various stages of the MEXT Scholarship.

https://mymextscholarship.com/

Past Embassy Language Proficiency and Other Tests

https://mymext.com/exams

Official MEXT and Japanese Government Resources

MEXT's Official Scholarship Webpage (Japanese)

Home to all official scholarship application guidelines, forms, and scholarship outline.
https://mymext.com/mextofficial

Study in Japan Official Application Guidelines Website: Graduate (English)

https://mymext.com/sijg

Study in Japan Official Application Guidelines Website: Undergraduate (English)

https://mymext.com/siju

List of Japanese Embassies and Consulates: Japanese Ministry of Foreign Affairs (English)

https://mymext.com/embassies

Government Statistics Cited in Text

e-Stat, "Number of International Students by Major (Graduate School)." Accessed December 26, 2023. https://www.e-stat.go.jp/stat-search/files?stat_infid=000031894030

e-Stat, "International students by nationality and associated department." Accessed December 27, 2023. https://www.e-stat.go.jp/stat-search/files?stat_infid=000040128667

Independent Administrative Institution Japan Student Services Organization, "Result of International Student Survey in Japan, 2023." Accessed June 9, 2024. https://www.studyinjapan.go.jp/en/_mt/2024/05/data2023z_e.pdf

Other Resources

VisualPing

VisualPing is a free tool for tracking changes to specific areas of websites, such as the MEXT page that shows the active scholarship applications. You can set a particular area of a site to review on a daily basis and Visual Ping will tell you if there are any changes to that section. I use this tool to let me know when the MEXT official website has released new guidelines.

https://visualping.io/

Japan Reference Forum

Forum with active discussions about the MEXT Scholarship application process each year.

https://mymext.com/jref

Reddit MEXT Scholarship Forum

https://mymext.com/redditmext